"We are glad to see a b
that Jesus' message of s
ognized more and more in a practical, vital way throughout
the Christian world. If everyone would read and understand
Two Hours to Freedom, churches and the people in them
would be transformed."

—from the foreword by **Francis and Judith MacNutt**,
founders and directors, Christian Healing Ministries

"Kraft shows a deep understanding of the spiritual and emotional roots of brokenness in the lives of many people, and
defines a clear path for ministry to them through the wisdom
of Scripture and power of the Holy Spirit. This is a resource
for pastoral counseling and spiritual intervention where sin
has produced strongholds of opposition to spiritual and
emotional healing."

—**Sherwood Lingenfelter**, Ph.D., provost and senior vice
president, professor of anthropology,
Fuller Theological Seminary

"Chuck Kraft offers a wealth of distilled practical wisdom
from his fruitful 25-year ministry of deep healing and deliverance. What an invaluable resource!"

—**Stephen A. Seamands**, Ph.D., professor of Christian
doctrine, Asbury Theological Seminary

"Chuck Kraft's work is an invaluable resource for those working with hurting people. *Two Hours to Freedom* describes a
practical, effective and balanced process."

—**John Shultz**, Ph.D., president,
Ashland Theological Seminary

"Far too many believers in Christ find their spiritual growth
blocked behind a dam of unrecognized and unresolved in-

juries and pain. Dr. Kraft's ministry has successfully demonstrated that emotional healing and spiritual growth can become a reality in a matter of hours, setting believers onto the path toward long-term freedom and maturity in their walks with Christ."

—**Doug Hayward**, Ph.D., professor of
intercultural studies, Biola University

"Once again Chuck Kraft makes one point abundantly clear: Jesus holds the power to heal the brokenhearted."

—**Terry Wardle**, D.Min., professor of practical theology,
director, Institute of Formational Counseling,
Ashland Theological Seminary

Two Hours to
FREEDOM

Two Hours to FREEDOM

A Simple and Effective Model for Healing and Deliverance

CHARLES H. KRAFT

Chosen

a division of Baker Publishing Group
Grand Rapids, Michigan

© 2010 by Charles H. Kraft

Published by Chosen Books
a division of Baker Publishing Group
P.O. Box 6287, Grand Rapids, MI 49516-6287
www.chosenbooks.com

Printed in the United States of America

Library of Congress Cataloging-in-Publication Data
Kraft, Charles H.
    Two hours to freedom : a simple and effective model for healing and deliverance / Charles H. Kraft.
        p.   cm.
    Includes bibliographical references and index.
    ISBN 978-0-8007-9498-9 (pbk.)
    1. Spiritual healing. 2. Prayer—Christianity. 3. Spiritual warfare. I. Title.
BT732.5.K74 2010
234′.131—dc22   2010017931

13   14   15   16   7   6   5   4   3

Contents

Foreword

After reading Charles Kraft's new book, we believe nearly everyone involved in the ministry of Christian healing prayer would profit by reading it. The very title *Two Hours to Freedom* reveals that Dr. Kraft is issuing a remarkable challenge. He believes that most Christians who suffer from deep inner and emotional problems can be freed after two hours of prayer using the principles he sets down here.

A psychotherapist by profession, I have seen the great value of Christian counseling but also, by and large, its limits. Counseling helps people with emotional problems to cope, but usually not to be freed, so I have a strong desire to read books like this one to learn about the amazing interior transformations that can come through prayer, which we have called inner healing. Dr. Kraft prefers the term *deep-level healing*. Francis and I hope Christian counselors can all experience adding healing prayers to counseling sessions to bring into reality the emotional and spiritual freedom that our clients long for.

Just this morning we received a letter from a man our ministry prayed for last week:

> Words in the English language seem insufficient to express my thanks to you. You may not know of the healing and deliverance I experienced through your loving prayer ministers. I feel somehow lighter in my being. Temptation to sin is still there, but it doesn't have the same hold. I'm still processing all that happened: the prayers, deliverance, blessings and anointing I received. I am writing with the utmost gratitude toward God, and sending to you grace, peace, love in the Lord and an abundance of God's blessings.

Over the years we have prayed for thousands of people suffering from spiritual and emotional wounds, as well as demonic complications, and rejoiced in the healings we have been privileged to witness. But ordinarily, for us, these healings came in stages, over a series of sessions, until total freedom came.

In this remarkable book Dr. Kraft shares a method of prayer that generally takes two hours (though he admits it used to take him longer). This is an extraordinary, positive claim, and Dr. Kraft has the credentials to make it. His teaching comes from a combination of study and the fruits of experience—more than 25 years in healing prayer ministry. We know him personally, moreover, as a thoughtful, rational and calm person, not given to hyperbole, and we believe his claim that ordinary Christians can expect deep results in two hours that will usually not require a return appointment.

Most of all, we are glad to see a book to add to the growing evidence that Jesus' message of setting the captives free is being recognized more and more in a practical, vital way throughout the Christian world.

We much appreciate Dr. Kraft's sharing of what he has learned—for example, that most spiritual and emotional wounds come down through the generations. The need for deep-level healing is so manifest in the Christian community that you can almost feel the heaviness that weighs people down who fill the church pews on Sunday morning.

If everyone would read and understand *Two Hours to Freedom*, churches and the people in them would be transformed.

Francis and Judith MacNutt
Founders and directors, Christian Healing Ministries
Jacksonville, Florida
www.christianhealingmin.org

Introduction

I have been involved in the ministry of inner healing since 1983. And I am totally convinced that this ministry is at the top of the list of all the things the Church needs. Jesus came to set captives free (Luke 4:18). He also said that we would carry on His ministry (John 14:12). But for the most part, unfortunately, the American Church has gotten lost in intellectualism and practices little or none of the ministry of freeing captives that Jesus modeled.

Many in the Church have worked under the delusion that simply coming to Christ brings healing. When we come to Christ, we are taught, "the old is gone, the new has come" (2 Corinthians 5:17). Therefore we do not have to pay attention to the internal stuff that keeps us bound—although if that stuff is bad enough there are professional counselors available to help us. What I have learned, however, is that healing is a step beyond salvation for many (probably most) Christians. Salvation is the necessary first step. But beyond it and built upon it is a second step—the healing step.

Inner or deep-level healing is a ministry that corrects that problem. It specializes in freeing people from the emotional and spiritual "garbage" we accumulate as we go through life. It frees people to be what Jesus intended us to be, and it frees the Church to be what it is supposed to be as well. The Church is intended to be a hospital, serving the Kingdom of God by healing people spiritually, emotionally and physically—like Jesus did.

Jesus said that when we see healing happening we will know that the Kingdom has come near (Luke 10:9). What if we don't see these things? Does that mean the Kingdom is not near? If so, the Kingdom is not near most of our churches.

As I state in the first chapter, it is as if God's people are in prisoner-of-war camps. They come into our churches seeking healing, but they are often told to "just suck it up" and made to feel that they shouldn't need healing once they have given their lives to Jesus. Their problems, however, do not just go away when they pray and try to forget them. So they blame themselves for the fact that they cannot simply give their problems to Jesus, adding another layer of guilt to the other areas in which they need healing.

These people need help. Some of them make their way to secular counselors or to Christian counselors who use similar methods, not having learned to work in prayer power during counseling sessions. Many Christian counselors have been intimidated by the American Psychological Association's rules and fear that they may lose their licenses if they introduce prayer or deal with demons in their practices. Without deliberately bringing the power of Jesus into the counseling relationship, they have only human power to solve superhuman problems. So it seldom works. People get help from those who practice secular counseling—but usually not healing.

Some of these persons come to me, get plugged into Jesus' power and go away with the newness they were promised when they came to Christ. This is not because I am so good but because Jesus comes to enable me to do things I cannot do. Deep-level healing is Jesus' healing. We start with Jesus, we continue with Jesus, we end with Jesus.

Jesus is the One who makes it work. I am just a midwife.

And you can do it, too. All you need in order to handle most of the cases that arise is Jesus and a few key techniques. Some cases might be beyond you; that's when you go to someone else for help. But you can bring freedom and healing to most of the people in your life.

The book in your hands is a small one, designed to be a kind of handbook for those who will take the risk and begin to minister deep-level healing. It is for people who (like me) are without spectacular gifting or charismatic credentials but who simply love Jesus and want to join Him in setting captives free.

I have, in essence, been "self-taught" in this ministry, but I am greatly indebted to those who have preceded me and to my contemporaries who have written and shared on this subject and accompanied me on the journey. I want to thank them and the folks at Chosen/Baker who have seen the book through to publication, especially Jane Campbell and Andrew Sloan.

May God bless you as you read, and may He lead you into setting captives free.

South Pasadena, California
February 2010

1

Where Things Start

Jane came to me with a problem I have heard many times. (Her name was not actually Jane; here, and throughout the book, I am using fictional names to protect the identity of my clients.) "I know I should be closer to Jesus," she said. "But as hard as I try, I don't seem to be able to get there."

Jane shared that she regularly read her Bible and prayed. And she attended church faithfully. She enjoyed worship. But something seemed to block her as she worshiped, leaving her frustrated and feeling that there must be something wrong with her. Others seemed to be able to get close to Jesus, especially in worship. But worship services left Jane disappointed and feeling guilty.

As we got into Jane's story, it was obvious that she had dealt with sin. She had confessed every sinful act and attitude she could think of and had accepted the forgiveness promised in 1 John 1:9. In addition, she had searched her memory for any people she needed to forgive and had forgiven them, as required by Jesus (see Matthew 6:14–15). Furthermore, as mentioned, she was diligent in personal and corporate spiritual disciplines. But the intimacy spoken of in John 15 eluded her.

I followed the ministry guidelines suggested in the following pages. And here's what I found: Inside Jane were "parts," which I have learned to call "inner children," that were hurting and fearful of intimacy. These parts, or inner children, had been neglected and mistreated by adults as Jane was growing up. And they now felt that grownup Jane was rejecting them, although she did not even know they were there.

Though adult Jane had worked hard at forgiving those who had neglected and mistreated her as a child, there was a lot of unforgiveness and hurt residing in the younger parts of her that did not go away when her adult self forgave. It was as if Jane's adult self had forgiven but her child parts had not. And this, as it turned out, was interfering with her intimacy with Jesus. She was blocked and in a kind of captivity—saved but not free.

Prisoner-of-War Camps

I believe that many in the Christian community, like Jane, live in spiritual "prisoner-of-war camps." Jesus said He came that we might have life—"life in all its fullness" or abundance (see John 10:10). And many have responded to Jesus' invitation and have gained eternal life though faith in Him. But the "in all its fullness" part escapes them. That is because fullness, or abundance, requires freedom. And for most people, gaining freedom is a step beyond the salvation step.[1]

When we come to Christ, the result is a "new being" or "new creature" (see 2 Corinthians 5:17). This newness, then, is a transformation of our innermost being, the part of us that we call our "spirit." The Holy Spirit comes to live in this part of us, and that is wonderful. We are saved for time and for eternity.

That is the good news. But there is bad news as well. We have four other parts that may not be transformed when we come to Christ. Most of us still have to fight to bring about transformation in our body, mind, emotions and will. These are the parts where such things as sin, hurts and un-Christian reactions and habits dwell, even after we come to Christ. And these parts, though they may undergo some change, rarely get transformed to the same extent as our spirit when we turn to Christ.

Unfortunately, this kind of dampened Christian experience is so pervasive among Christians that it is considered normal. But Jesus intended the Christian life to be so much more: life in its fullness, life in its abundance, life that does not hurt, life that does not make us long for heaven in order to escape a Christianity that has not lived up to the promises of Scripture.

People Have Problems

So, people have problems, most of which are spiritual and emotional. We are often good at hiding them from both others and ourselves. But they are there. And they keep us from the freedom we seek internally and from the intimacy with Christ that we read about in the Scriptures.

Jesus said, "I am the vine, and you are the branches. Those who remain in me, and I in them, will bear much fruit; for you can do nothing without me" (John 15:5). We might easily assume that producing "fruit" refers to winning people to Christ. But in the context of John 15, what Jesus was promising was an internal meaningfulness that comes only when internal hindrances are eliminated.

Later Jesus prayed to the Father:

> May they be in us, just as you are in me and I am in you. . . .
> I in them and you in me, so that they may be completely one,
> in order that the world may know that you sent me and that
> you love them as you love me.
>
> John 17:21–23

Jesus' goal was that we be as close to Him as He is to the Father. But this requires freedom, and life's hurts and offenses get in our way. We have come in faith to Jesus, so our eternal destiny is assured. Most Christians, however, are still blocked, as was Jane. Saved but not free.

Jesus said He came to bring good news to the poor, to proclaim liberty to the captives and to set free the oppressed (see Luke 4:18). Freedom was a major theme of His ministry: freedom in the face of captivity and oppression. And the "poor" Jesus was referring to were those who felt that God was not on their side, that He was either neglecting them or punishing them.

When we come to Christ for salvation we gain an eternal spiritual freedom that is the most valuable thing in our lives. But for many—perhaps most—Christians, the freedom of salvation does not feel like all that was promised when they were attracted to a relationship with Jesus. In fact, it seems as though a large number of truly born again Christians are still living in emotional and spiritual captivity, in prisoner-of-war camps. I have had a steady stream of committed Christians, like Jane, come to me for ministry with the complaint that they do not feel free and they do not feel close to Jesus, even after all He has done for them.

As I minister to these people, we inevitably find issues in their past that have resulted in emotional and spiritual wounds to which they are captive. If these were physical problems, a doctor would first deal with the wounds and then put a cast or a large bandage on them. However, we often try to get emotional or spiritual problems healed by putting casts or bandages on them without first dealing with the wounds. As with physical problems, the wound or root cause of the problem needs to be dealt with if the person is to be healed. Approaches that ignore or superficially deal with the problem do not bring healing because they do not deal with the root cause of the wound.

Some of the problems with which people come to me are caused by sin. But more are the result of emotional damage that has occurred, often so early in life that the person can recall the events only with difficulty, if at all. Sin is not the issue with these problems, though they are often caused by people sinning against my client. Emotional and spiritual damage is the issue.

Most people need deep-level healing because they have experienced inner emotional and spiritual damage during the course of their lives. Unfortunately, there is little attempt to deal with such problems within our churches. And the amount of healing available through secular counseling is limited, and generally comes at great monetary cost.

The Answer

I believe the answer lies in what has been called "inner healing." I prefer to call it "deep-level healing," since we are attempting to bring healing to persons at the deepest level. And our deepest level is emotional and spiritual.

By way of definition, deep-level healing is a ministry in the power of the Holy Spirit aimed at bringing healing to the whole person: spirit, body, mind, emotions and will. Since the deepest hurts are stored in memories, we focus there, seeking to apply the power of Jesus to the roots of a person's problems. Since demons are usually involved in deep-level problems, we are concerned with getting people free of them as well. But demons are secondary; the "garbage" they are attached to is primary. Thus, our approach is to deal with the root spiritual and emotional issues first, weakening any demons that may be attached, then to cast out the demons.

We do not ignore the demons, even though they are a secondary problem. Nor do we assume, as some ministries do, that if the inner stuff is dealt with the demons will go away on their own. This seldom, if ever, happens. We deal with the garbage and then tackle the demons, casting them out as Jesus did. And we seldom have any demonic demonstrations such as those Hollywood is fond of showing.

Jesus has given us the authority and power to work with Him to set captives free (see Luke 9:1). We believe, then, that the ministry of deep-level healing is intended by Jesus to be a primary ministry of the Church.

Who Needs Deep-Level Healing?

There are several categories of people who are in need of deep-level healing and several types of problems to address. The first category of people consists of those who sin by holding on to negative attitudes toward others, toward themselves and/or toward God. It is sin, in the end, that is the problem. To adequately deal with the sin in our lives, however, our definition of sin needs to be much broader than the usual definitions. It will include holding on to such emotional reactions as unforgiveness, anger, hatred, bitterness, resentment, fear, shame, guilt, self-rejection, self-hatred, death wishes and many other attitudes that negatively affect our relationship with God.

Such attitudes usually arise when people react to someone sinning against them. When people are physically, emotionally or sexually abused, they naturally react in anger. But such a reaction is not a sin (see Ephesians 4:26). It is the holding of the anger, allowing it to become unforgiveness, that is sinful and internally damaging. When such reactions are ignored, they fester and cause problems more serious than the original wounds. They become infected and refuse to go away.

Those who have intentionally or unintentionally harbored such attitudes need freedom from the internal damage produced by them. For example, someone harboring unforgiveness and anger or hatred over a period of time sustains great emotional damage, and in addition gets infested with demons. Such was the case of a woman in her mid-thirties who had lived for most of her life with an intense hatred toward her father. That hatred (which, by the way, her father rightly deserved) had caused a severe case of diabetes and resulting blindness, as well as digestive problems that required a colostomy.

Those who harbor negative attitudes toward themselves constitute a second major group who need deep-level healing. Many people suffer from self-condemnation, self-rejection and even self-loathing. In spite of the value God puts on us, a value we often know only in our heads, our feelings toward ourselves may be quite negative. Frequently the roots of such attitudes lie in the fact that we were not wanted as children. Much of Jane's self-rejection appeared to be rooted in her mother's attitude while Jane was in the womb. Abuse during childhood or adolescence is another frequent source of self-hatred.

Thirdly, many people are holding anger toward God. These individuals, too, need deep-level healing. They often reason that, since God is all-powerful, the fact that He allowed them to experience bad things must mean He doesn't love them. Like Job, they feel that God is unreasonable and capricious. They fail to see the extent to which God has limited Himself by granting free will to humans and to Satan.

The Presence of Demons

A further set of reasons for needing deep-level healing stems from the activity of demons in human life. We will go into more detail on this in chapter 5, but should mention here that demons take advantage of people by attaching themselves to the emotional and spiritual garbage that is already there. They then become a part of the emotional and spiritual garbage we have to confront. The major job of demons is to attach themselves to the garbage in order to make bad things worse. They try to cripple anyone they can—and harass those they cannot cripple. They are especially concerned with crippling or harassing Christians, lest we discover the power God has given us and become a threat to their activities.

In addition to the emotional and spiritual "garbage" to which demonic "rats" can attach themselves, demons can be inherited. Many people have individuals in their ancestry who have given themselves to Satan through participation in occult organizations or through dedications to the gods or spirits of their ancestors. Family spirits and other spirits are regularly passed down through bloodlines. I would estimate that well over half the people I have cast demons out of have had at least one inherited demon.

And then there are the increasing number of people who have themselves made commitments to spirits through involvement in New Age or other occult organizations. These also need deep-level healing.

Furthermore, many have been cursed or have cursed themselves. I work with missionaries a lot, and I often find that someone in their area of service has cursed them. Children who are not wanted often carry a curse of unwantedness, consciously or unconsciously put on them by their parents. Self-cursing is often engaged in during adolescence by teenagers who are not pleased with the way their bodies look or are developing. "I hate my _____" constitutes a curse, and frequently is all the legal right a demon needs to enter and live in that person.

So, Let's Seek Freedom

Most of the people who come to see me are keenly aware of their sins, according to the narrower definition of sin used by most Christians. And they have confessed those sins to God, sometimes over and over, but often have little sense of release. They come knowing in their heads that they are forgiven, but not feeling free. The reason is usually found in the fact that their wounds have emotional and/or spiritual roots that do not go away simply through repentance.

It is the roots that I seek to deal with, then, in ministry. I assume that present issues have roots, usually early in life, and that if we can bring healing to those roots the present feelings and behavior will be affected positively.

Ellie had been in deep depression for nearly a year. Her condition was so severe that she was about to be sent home from her missionary assignment. We found that she had been burdened with adult responsibilities very early in life and had developed a deep sense of resentment toward life and authority. Because of this she carried resentment toward her family, her mission and life in general. But she had no idea where the resentment had come from until we invited Jesus into her childhood memories.

As I guided Ellie to experience with mental pictures the deep love and care of Jesus, she began to feel something quite different. It was freedom, but she did not recognize it at first. Ellie was able to give to Jesus the heaviness she had been carrying. But the new feeling was so unfamiliar that she thought she was back in depression! Though she had given her life to Jesus years ago, she had never felt freedom until this moment.

It is for people like Ellie that I write this book. People come to me for two hours at a time; and we go back to childhood memories, starting at conception. I invite them to meet Jesus, rejoicing with Him in the good memories and giving Him their damaged feelings in the bad memories. And He releases them from the emotional and spiritual drag they have never been able to overcome on their own. Two hours to freedom!

Jesus' Power Can Bring Freedom

Whether from emotional, spiritual or demonic problems, then, people need freedom. Unfortunately, the spiritual blindness of Western Christianity provides little help in dealing with these issues. Many pastors and other Christian leaders have gotten into the habit of referring people who struggle with emotional problems to professional counselors—most of whom, though they may be Christians, are practicing secular counseling. Some get help from these counselors. But many are disappointed, since there often is little, if any, real healing power in secular counseling. People often learn what to call their problems and how to live with them, but they seldom receive the healing and freedom they have expected as a result of their relationship with Jesus.

To underline the ineffectiveness of professional counseling we need look no further than the studies of those who research such results from within the psychological community.[2]

Some of these studies show that professional counseling is better at providing support for people with their problems than it is at getting the problems healed. Many who come to me attest to that fact. I believe the reason is that there is not enough healing power in psychological technique. I believe the reason is that, as impressive as the knowledge and techniques of psychology are, there is not enough healing power in them. Only Jesus can supply the power we need to gain genuine freedom.

One major problem those who do secular counseling face, as I mentioned in the Introduction, is that they may lose their licenses if they are found to be dealing with demonization. So even those counselors who believe in demonization steer clear of it for fear of the American Psychological Association, or avoid demonization because they have not been taught how to handle it.

I have great respect for psychology and for professional counselors. However, a steady stream of clients come to me who are profoundly disappointed in the results of the time and money they have invested in professional counseling. Most of them value the help they have received, especially if the counselor is a Christian, but complain that they have not been healed—their problems are still there, though better controlled.

The Holy Spirit can and does use Christians practicing secular counseling. But my clients raise questions about its effectiveness. Very few of those who have spent two hours or more with me have the same complaints. The typical response is rejoicing in newfound freedom, even after months or years have passed.

Perhaps here is the place to mention that there are those who suffer from genuine mental health issues (as opposed to emotional and spiritual issues). Though God occasionally heals such people directly, they seldom are helped through inner healing. Their problems are biological, and their capacity to deal with emotional and spiritual issues is diminished. These individuals need professional help and medication to stabilize them so they can cope with life. Inner healers can sometimes help if these clients have the mental capacity to allow us to deal with emotions and demonization, but they need to be referred to professionals to handle most of their problems.

For most people, though, the issues are emotional and spiritual rather than biological. They need freedom, and the Church has been commissioned by Jesus to bring that freedom (see Galatians 1:4; 5:1). I aim in this book to show the way, through deep-level healing, to deal with these problems.

This book is intended to be a guidebook for those who want to bring freedom to others. But no doubt some who read it will be yearning for healing themselves. Though deep-level healing does not by any means fit into the category of "self-help," I trust that this book will help those who need healing to have a better understanding of relevant issues—and especially to gain hope for experiencing God's gift of freedom. For their sake, I have included in Appendix B on pages 161–63 a list of inner healing ministries located throughout the United States, with some overseas. This list will also provide an opportunity for people who do this kind of ministry to connect with others.

As we move toward the chapter in which I outline my "Two Hours to Freedom" approach, in chapter 2 we will first detail some of the emotional and spiritual problems with which we need to deal. In chapter 3 we will consider some fascinating insights about our memories and how those insights can be incorporated into the healing process. Next in chapter 4 we will focus on working with our inner selves, where hurts are stored. Then in chapter 5 we will turn to the subject of demons and demonization. All of this leads to chapter 6—"Two Hours to Freedom"—where I will present my usual approach to freeing people. (In Appendix A you can find the questionnaire I have people fill out before this ministry session, plus, in Appendix B, a list of inner healing ministries.) The final chapter examines our habits, an important follow-up after a person's painful roots have been healed.

I am confident that you are reading this book because you want to see genuine and lasting change, through the power of the Holy Spirit, in people's lives. Walk with me now as we lay the foundation for two hours of transformational ministry into which we—working with the Holy Spirit, and whether or not we have spectacular gifting—can lead people.

2

Problems to Deal With

Eric came to me with a typical set of male issues. He was angry. Since our society allows most men that one negative emotion, Eric was aware of his anger. What he was not aware of was that he was also fearful, ashamed, carrying a lot of guilt and feeling rejected. All of these things and more came out as we got into his story. His parents had favored his older brother and younger sister. Eric struggled academically in high school and college, though he did excel in football and track.

Eric got married soon after he graduated from college, and he and Heidi were blessed to have two children. Unfortunately, Heidi came to live in fear of Eric's frequent outbursts of rage. He had never gotten violent with his wife or children, but they were afraid of him and felt like they were walking on eggshells whenever he was home.

Eric did well in his job, attended church regularly with his family and appeared to be a model husband and father. But his wife and children knew another side of him. And now

Heidi had threatened to leave him if he did not get help. She had made such threats before, but something about the way she said it this time convinced Eric that she meant business. Besides, Eric himself wanted to be able to control his anger and save his marriage.

Eric emailed me for an appointment, and I scheduled two hours for us to meet together. As we talked about his childhood, Eric shared that his father had a wicked temper and that Eric could never seem to satisfy him. Since he was the second son and felt that his parents favored his sister, I asked Eric if he felt that his parents wanted him. We also explored a number of other indicators that led to Eric's feelings that he was unwanted.

I then asked Jesus to take Eric back to the womb. He found himself quite uncomfortable during the exercise, feeling that he was not supposed to have been conceived. It helped, though, for him to meet Jesus in his prebirth memories and to hear that any rejection he was feeling was his parents' problem, not his. Jesus assured Eric of the truth of my words that he was where he was supposed to be, that Jesus was with him and that he did not need to feel guilty about being a disappointment to his parents. That was their problem, not his. I then spoke to this younger, prebirth part of Eric to let him know that Jesus wanted him to be there, that he was going to make it to adulthood and that the next child his mother would have would be the girl his parents had wanted.

Next I asked Eric if he could forgive his parents. Speaking for his preborn inner child, Eric forgave his parents for wanting him to be a girl.

Thus we began the two-hour ministry session outlined in the following chapters, and Eric got free. There were further problems that emerged as we went along—each of Eric's inner children had to forgive his parents, and others, and give their anger, shame, fear and rejection to Jesus. Eric got rid of his "garbage" during our session and returned to his family a radically changed person who, though he still had a bit of work to do to change a lifetime of habits, never again scared his family with outbursts of rage.

Spiritual Factors

The first set of problems to deal with in order to arrive at deep-level healing are the spiritual factors that lead to problems at this level. The emotional and spiritual areas of life are so intertwined that deficiencies in one area tend to spill over into the other. Spiritual deficiencies may produce symptoms that are or at least appear to be emotional. We will attempt to distinguish spiritual from emotional factors whenever possible, though the two are often intertwined.

There are at least seven factors contributing to spiritual deficiencies. Each of these can lead to what appear to be emotional symptoms.

1. *Sin is a leading cause of spiritual woundedness.* Though most people who come to me, as I have mentioned, have been diligent about dealing with sin problems, we cannot ignore them. Scripture tells us that we are full of all types of sin (see Galatians 5:19–21). Our fallen human nature ("flesh") is no good (see Jeremiah 17:9; Romans 7:18). Left to our own devices we naturally do wrong. There is a battle between the spirit and the flesh. Each time we give in to our flesh we weaken ourselves spiritually. Our relationship with God is disrupted until we confess our sins and receive His forgiveness (see 1 John 1:9).

People cannot be free and healed without dealing with sin. Sin, however, is much broader than we usually think of it. The essence of sin is disobedience to God. And disobedience to God is automatically obedience to Satan, God's enemy. When Adam and Eve disobeyed God and obeyed Satan, they lost their freedom. Likewise, when we disobey God we move into what we may call "unfreedom," or captivity.

In the discussion that follows we will deal extensively with emotional issues such as anger, shame, guilt, self-rejection and a desire to die. All of these, as well as more obvious things like lying, adultery and idolatry, are sins if we wallow in them. However, since the theological term "sin" is often misunderstood, I use it sparingly. I choose, instead, to focus on the specific activity (anger, adultery, guilt, etc.) rather than risk being misinterpreted.

2. *Neglecting our relationship with God also weakens us spiritually.* God created us for relationship with Him. Intimacy with God means spending time with Him. Jesus, our example, frequently withdrew to spend time alone with the Father (see Matthew 14:13; Mark 1:35). If Jesus needed to spend time alone with the Father, so do we. This feeds our spirit.

A typical way of spending time with God is by setting aside time daily to read and meditate on Scripture and to pray. I would also recommend that we do a lot of picturing. I will discuss the value of picturing later. Suffice it to say here that this is a more tangible way of experiencing the presence of Jesus. He is omnipresent and has promised to be with us always (see Matthew 28:20), so when we picture Him with us we are picturing the truth.

We can picture Jesus present with us in our daily activities. We can picture ourselves in the events of Scripture. We can picture Jesus with us in events that are planned but not yet experienced.

Worship is another way of spending time with Jesus. Jesus loves it and Satan hates it when we worship. The contemporary worship movement has been a great help to getting our feelings into gear in our relating to Jesus.

3. *A wrong view of God can lead to spiritual sickness.* Some people perceive God to be harsh because their earthly father has been harsh. They see Him as ready to pounce on them the moment they make a wrong move in life. One woman I ministered to told me that whenever she pictured Jesus she saw Him with a stick in His hands, ready to discipline her.

Some are angry with God because they experienced abuse that they believe He could have stopped. Still others see God as being distant and unconcerned about them.

Such views participate in a satanic deceit, seeing Jesus as opposed to us even though He did so much for us. Jesus is on our side (see Romans 8:31). He gave Himself for us to deal with our sins, as well as our emotional and spiritual wounds. These faulty perceptions lead to seriously flawed interpretations as to why Christians have difficulties in their lives. People with such views fail to see that God has put certain limitations on Himself by giving humans free will. Plus, He has not promised to keep us from life's difficulties, though He has promised to be with us in the midst of them (see Matthew 28:20; John 16:33; Acts 14:22; Philippians 1:29).

We may not understand why Jesus allowed certain things in our lives, but we cannot accuse Him of being against us or of being unconcerned about us. If we make such accusations, we are committing serious sin.

4. *A related misconception concerning God often results in anger at God.* People often assume that since God is omnipotent He can do anything He wants to do at any time He wants to do it. Deterministic theologies such as extreme

Calvinism often lead to this error. People affected by such theologies do not realize that by giving humans free will God has allowed the choice a human makes to be the final verdict. Therefore, God often does not get what He wants. For example, it is not His will that any perish (see 2 Peter 3:9), yet the final choice of many is to turn their backs on Him, thus denying God what He wants. If God got His way, everyone would be saved. But God allows humans to make the final choice that leads either to heaven or to hell.

God cannot be limited by anything outside Himself. In this sense He is omnipotent. However, He can limit Himself. And He has chosen to limit Himself by giving humans free will. His will is always to save, but He saves only those who agree; and He honors the choice of those who refuse His offer. He seems to have made a rule for Himself not to choose anyone who does not agree to choose Him.

In His working with humans, then, another of God's rules seems to be that He will not work in the human arena without human partners. It is up to humans to choose whether they will partner with God or with Satan. When we partner with God, His work gets done. When we do not partner with God, the things He wants do not get done. When people partner with Satan, they use their free will to hurt other people. We cannot, therefore, blame God for the hurts we sustain. The responsibility lies with the people who have misused the free will God gave them.

Satan has to obey the same rule. He entices people to partner with him to do his will, much of which is destructive to humans. People who have been victimized by those who partner with Satan often feel that God has abandoned and neglected them. Such flawed perceptions result in people wallowing in anger, bitterness and unforgiveness toward God Himself.

While God ultimately accomplishes His purposes, people have often lost sight of the fact that He involves humans in His plans. Note, for example, that the best translation of Romans 8:28 is "in all things God works for good *with those who love him*" (emphasis added). He does not carry out His plans all by Himself. When people partner with Him, those plans move forward. But many things do not go God's way as He seeks to work in partnership with humans toward ultimate victory. For many use their free will to obey Satan rather than to obey God, to hurt rather than to help. So it is the human factor, when people choose to partner with Satan, that does the hurting, not God.

God has been let down, even by His own people, more times than we could ever imagine. And this makes it look as if He does not care, since He does not stop many abusive things done by one human to another. The fact that God has limited Himself in relationships with both humans and Satan is difficult to explain to hurting people. Yet, though the enemy's goal is to destroy us, it is God working in the background, limiting the enemy's activities, that enables us to survive. We wish it to be different, that God would be more overt in fighting for us. But He has chosen to do things this way, suffering with us in those things that challenge us—in the background, all the while, setting limitations on what Satan or humans can do to us so that things are not as bad as they could be (see 1 Corinthians 10:13).

5. *A fifth cause of spiritual sickness is satanic harassment.* There seem to be laws of the universe that give rights to the enemy. If there are spiritual, emotional or mental problems in a person's life (the things we are calling "garbage"), the enemy can attack that person. The enemy does not originate such problems; he merely takes advantage of them. Like rats are attracted to garbage, our enemy is attracted to wounds that

are already there. Our wounds are the garbage, and demons are the rats. The enemy likes to harass us by taking advantage of already existing things such as fear, guilt, anger and lust. His attacks on such problem areas can disrupt sleep and other normal functions such as prayer, worship and Bible study.

Some attacks may involve curses or vows. Proverbs 26:2 speaks of curses not being able to land or have impact without a reason. The implication is that if there is a reason, then they can have an impact. I believe a lot of cursing goes on, most of which is informal, such as words spoken in anger (e.g., *I hate my hips*) that are empowered by the forces of darkness. Sometimes the cursing is initiated by formal procedures or reinforced by a ritual. Such curses are more powerful. Either way, if the curses hit their mark they will be experienced as satanic attack. The good news is that such curses can usually be broken easily when we take authority over them and cancel them in Jesus' name.

When people are angry with themselves they often say such things as *I hate myself* (or *I hate my body* or *I hate my name*), or *I wish that part of me wasn't so* _____, or *I vow not to be like my father* or *I vow not to be like my mother*. When we say such things against ourselves, we often find that the enemy sneaks in and empowers the words, making them curses or vows. He thus gains the right to harass.

Breaking self-curses or vows is usually a relatively simple process. It usually involves saying something like "In the name of Jesus Christ I renounce any curses I have made against myself or any part of me and any vows I have made that are empowered by Satan." The person who makes the curse or vow has the authority to cancel it.

We can usually break curses that have come from someone else by saying something like "In the name of Jesus I return this curse to its sender as a blessing." We are commanded to bless those who curse us (see Romans 12:14). If this fails to break the curse, we need to find someone who knows how to break curses to help us.

6. *A sixth cause is demonization, evil spirits living within a person.* It is quite common in deep-level healing to have to deal with demons living in people. Note that we do not use the mistranslation "demon-possessed." There is no warrant for that translation; the New Testament wording simply means "to have a demon."[1]

When people who have demons become Christians, the demons must move out of their spirit but can reside in other parts of them. As a new believer grows in faith and deals with the spiritual and emotional garbage to which demons have become attached, the demons are weakened and suppressed and their ability to influence the individual diminishes. But they seldom leave until they are cast out. While many Christians have been able to get rid of demons living within themselves, the help of someone who knows how to cast them out is usually required. We will deal with this important subject in chapter 5.

7. *Demonization can come from generational spirits or curses.* We can inherit spirits or be subject to vows that took place long before we were even born. Exodus 20:5–6 may be speaking of spiritual inheritance, saying that the punishment for sins can be passed on to descendants to the third and fourth generation. If verse 5 implies generational spirits, it suggests that their effects may be limited to three or four generations. Many of the generational spirits I have had to cast out, however, claimed to have been in families for many more than three or four generations.

The fact is that people who have become demonized through their own willful participation in occult organizations pass these demons on to their children and, through them, to succeeding generations. Freemasons, Scientologists, followers of New Age and other occultists curse themselves and their families, allowing demonic infestation to be passed from generation to generation. Family spirits resulting from the dedication of infants in past generations also get inherited.

I have found that almost every type of demon can be passed on through inheritance. This often manifests itself in persons showing the same negative emotional characteristics as their ancestors, these having been passed on demonically. I have found what seem to be inherited spirits of fear, death, pornography, rejection, hate, rage, homosexuality, cancer and diabetes attached to just about any other human problem.

There seem to be generational bondages, often (perhaps always) reinforced by demons, in which particular sins or compulsions occur generation after generation. In these instances we have the authority to renounce such bondages if they are in us and to cancel them in others. People can be in bondage to Satan due to such things as contemporary or generational curses, self-curses and authority relationships that create what we call "soul ties." These result from satanic empowerment of relationships in which one person is dominated by another or has had an extramarital sexual relationship with another.

Many non-Western peoples (including Native Americans) routinely dedicate their children to clan or tribal gods and spirits before or at birth. Chinese, Korean and Japanese parents and grandparents traditionally take a written record of the date and time of birth of a newborn to a temple to be blessed by, and dedicated to, a god. While their intent is to gain protection and blessing for the child, they are actually putting him or her under the authority of evil spirits.

Emotional Factors

Though the distinction between spiritual factors and emotional factors is far from clear, the following list focuses on reactions that are expressed emotionally, whether or not they are also spiritual.

1. *The first thing to recognize is the fact that reactions, even more than the abuse in focus, usually cause the most damage.* Though abuse, whether physical, emotional or sexual, can cause great damage to a person, his or her *reactions* to that abuse are often even more damaging. For example, if an individual has been physically abused as a child, especially by a parent, there are significant hurts stemming from the mistreatment that need healing. The emotional and spiritual reaction of unforgiveness, however, is likely to be an even more crippling problem.

It is significant, in this regard, that whenever Jesus mentioned dealing with the hurts of life His command was to forgive. To forgive is to give up our right to take revenge on those who hurt us. Jesus' constant message was to forgive and to leave revenge to Him. And as Paul said in Romans 12:19, revenge is God's prerogative. Both in the Sermon on the Mount and the parable of the unforgiving servant, Jesus' frightening message was that if we do not forgive those who have hurt us we will not be forgiven by God for the sins we have committed (see Matthew 6:14–15; 18:32–35).

It is inevitable that we react to the events that occur during the course of our lives. Life is difficult, even for those raised in a good home. People experience sickness, they may experience parental neglect, they may have been conceived out of wedlock or, like Eric, they may be the "wrong" sex. Whatever the misfortune, the reaction must be addressed.

When hurt, our response is often to suppress the emotion and "bandage" the wound so that no one can see it. But when a wound has not been cleansed it festers. As time passes the bandage begins to leak the infection. This allows the experiences that took place years ago to influence our present life.

Negative life experiences are especially strong in their ability to impact a person's physical, emotional and spiritual health. They normally affect relationships—with God, self and others—in a major way. Then, under strong satanic influence, people tend to blame themselves for their difficulties, even when it is not their fault. Victims almost always blame themselves for their problems.

2. *One reaction that the enemy is particularly active in promoting is to get us to turn against ourselves.* Such negative attitudes toward ourselves are frequently the reaction to hurts received from those close to us. For example, as children we assume that our parents know what they are doing. Therefore, if they seem to be against us we assume it must be because there is something wrong with us. It never occurs to us until we get older that how our parents treated us might be because of something wrong with *them*. We blame ourselves and become victimizers who victimize ourselves.

Many people dislike and even hate themselves. I had this problem. It usually shows itself in a person's "self-talk." When we go around repeating to ourselves such things as *How stupid!* or *You fool—you'll never amount to anything* or *You'll never get it right* or *There you go again*, it is not surprising that our internal lives are deeply affected by the negativity. Such comments usually become self-curses. And they are often the habitual repetition of things that others have said to us. Additional commonly heard expressions are

Shame on you! or *You ought to be ashamed of yourself!* We simply continue what was begun by someone else.

Our self-esteem is one of the primary targets of the enemy. That is where his strongest attacks are often aimed. He does not want us to know who we are. The enemy tries his best to keep us from feeling—and if possible, from even knowing— that we are created in God's image (see Genesis 1:26) and that, if we are in Christ, we are in God (see Colossians 3:3), redeemed (see Galatians 3:13), a new being or creation (see 2 Corinthians 5:17), a child of God (see John 1:12–13; 1 John 3:1), a royal priesthood (see 1 Peter 2:9), holy (see 1 Corinthians 1:2), a joint heir with Christ (see Romans 8:17), a citizen of heaven (see John 1:12; Ephesians 2:6; Philippians 3:20) and a saint in whom the Holy Spirit dwells (see Galatians 4:6). The enemy wants to steal all such recognition from us. He is out to destroy us, and one of his major tactics is to keep us thinking about how sinful, fat, skinny, stupid, weak, ugly, pathetic or hopeless we are.

Satan even tried to mess with Jesus' self-esteem when he kept using the word "if" to challenge Jesus as he tempted Him. Twice he said, "*If* you are God's Son . . ." (see Luke 4:3, 9), as if to cause Jesus to doubt who He was. Satan was challenging Jesus to prove to Himself and to everyone else who He was.

Researchers have found that people have a better and more accurate memory of negative things than of positive things.[2] Before this was discovered, David Seamands wrote,

People will remember a single hurtful criticism most vividly while tending to forget a string of compliments. And they will feel a positive or a negative statement about what they *are* much more deeply than one concerning what they *did.* Thus, it's easy to see why the put-downs of being can be so completely shattering to our self-esteem.[3]

Part of the problem has to do with the fact that our subconscious is like a journalist who records all information coming in without regard to whether it is true. We then continue the abuse by running these statements through our minds over and over, so that by the time we reach adulthood we need deep-level healing to correct this.

3. *There are a number of significant emotional reactions that keep coming up as I minister to people.* The first of these is *anger.*

When hurt, individuals tend to respond with anger, resentment and a desire for revenge. These reactions enable them to survive at the time of the hurt. While such reactions are natural and legitimate, they become a problem for the person who hangs on to them. They often turn into bitterness and even depression. These attitudes create a significant amount of the garbage mentioned previously. Again, the event is not usually as much of a problem as the reaction related to it. These attitudes can lead to illness in any or all areas of a person's life. They can also provide opportunity for demonic harassment and invasion.

God gave us anger as a release. Anger is not in and of itself a sin. It is when we fail to let go of the anger that we are at risk. We see this in the apostle Paul's letter to the Ephesians:

> If you become angry, do not let your anger lead you into sin, and do not stay angry all day. Don't give the Devil a chance. . . . Get rid of all bitterness, passion, and anger. No more shouting or insults, no more hateful feelings of any sort. Instead, be kind and tender-hearted to one another, and forgive one another, as God has forgiven you through Christ.
>
> Ephesians 4:26–27, 31–32

The problem, then, is not the angry reaction itself but whether we keep the anger. Jesus Himself got angry on more than one occasion (see Matthew 11:20–24; 16:23; 21:12–13, 19; 23:13; John 2:13–17). But He refused to hang on to anger. He did not give the devil a chance to feed on the garbage of continuing anger and unforgiveness.

God knows how damaging it is for us to hold on to anger. He has called us to forgive, *to give up our right to revenge.* Paul writes, "Never take revenge, my friends, but instead let God's anger do it. For the scripture says, 'I will take revenge, I will pay back, says the Lord'" (Romans 12:19). Indeed, there is no peace without forgiveness.

Once we have made a choice to release anger, we still need to protect our minds by developing the proper attitude. The enemy launches all types of assaults on our minds, trying to get us to react by dwelling on negative things rather than on positive things. Yet Scripture tells us,

> Fill your minds with those things that are good and that deserve praise: things that are true, noble, right, pure, lovely, and honorable. . . . And the God who gives us peace will be with you.
>
> Philippians 4:8–9

After processing an event and deciding on an action such as forgiveness, we need to move on. Dwelling on the negative is a habit that many people desperately need to break. Healing involves changing our thoughts each time we find ourselves dwelling on the negative, until we are no longer doing so.

4. *A second emotional reaction that needs to be dealt with is shame, with its siblings guilt and deception.* I define *shame* simply as feeling bad about who we are. Such an attitude

45

feeds right into the self-esteem problems discussed earlier. The enemy, of course, works over anyone he can with shame issues, often using parents and other significant others to articulate messages such as "Shame on you!" or "You ought to be ashamed of yourself!"

One of Satan's strategies is to keep people mired in shame and/or guilt over sins committed, confessed and forgiven. He questions Jesus' forgiveness on the basis of our confession alone. "After what you've done," he says, "do you think you can get out of it that easy?" Satan says such things and teaches us to repeat them to ourselves, thus infecting our internal habits in a big way.

Satan's preferred way of pushing shame and guilt on us is through deception. Deception is not the same as lying. It is much more subtle, sometimes even using truth to deceive. Satan did not lie to Adam and Eve in the Garden of Eden when he said, "You will not die" (see Genesis 3:4). He simply referred to a different death—physical death that would not affect them for years. But Satan certainly deceived by referring to a different death than God had spoken of in Genesis 2:17. His deception had the ring of truth and was effective.

When the devil uses statements like those above to shame us, he is deceiving us. Satan is called a liar (see John 8:44). But more than that he is a deceiver. And when there is abuse—verbal, physical or sexual—he deceives us into believing that we deserve such treatment. So we live with the guilt and shame as if we had invited the abuse and were not worthy of being protected.

So, as we see, the enemy likes to focus on the fact that we are sinners and that failure is the most prominent characteristic in our lives. Taking a bit of truth and exaggerating its importance is one of his most effective strategies. When we view our sin as so big we often miss the confidence Jesus put in His disciples—and, by extension, in us—in spite of their continual doubt, lack of faith and failure. In Scripture, the fact that we are sinners is a minor theme compared to the emphasis on who God has created and called us to be. The major theme is articulated in exalted language in Romans:

> If God is for us, who can be against us? Certainly not God, who did not even keep back his own Son, but offered him for us all! He gave us his Son—will he not also freely give us all things? Who will accuse God's chosen people? God himself declares them not guilty! Who, then, will condemn them? Not Christ Jesus, who died, or rather, who was raised to life and is at the right side of God, pleading with him for us! Who, then, can separate us from the love of Christ? Can trouble do it, or hardship or persecution or hunger or poverty or danger or death? . . . No, in all these things we have complete victory through him who loved us!

Romans 8:31–35, 37

Paul proclaims the truth in direct contradiction of the enemy's lies that are aimed at disinheriting us from the position in which God has placed us. We are God's children, entitled to all the rights and privileges of family members. We can cooperate with our enemy and ignore this fact, but nothing can take it away from us. When we enter the freedom God has for us we can hold our heads high, knowing in our innermost being that who we are to God is who we are to ourselves. Shame and guilt are no longer our masters.

5. *Fear, and its comrades worry, anxiety and panic, are the next set of reactions to tackle.* As with anger, it is not a sin to react in fear on occasion, but it is a sin to hold on to it. Fear can be a tough taskmaster and a worthy servant of Satan. There is much teaching and exhortation countering

fear in the Scriptures. One of the best examples is found in Isaiah 41:10: "Do not be afraid—I am with you! I am your God—let nothing terrify you! I will make you strong and help you; I will protect you and save you."

Warnings about worrying are a major theme of Jesus' Sermon on the Mount. We are not to worry about food and clothing or about the future (see Matthew 6:25–34). God will take care of these things for us, just as He does for the rest of the physical creation. Our enemy, of course, delights to see us anxious and fearful over the imagined challenges of life and exercised over things we cannot control. But worry and fear are anti-faith reactions. The appropriate reaction for a Christian is to "Leave all your worries with [God], because he cares for you" (1 Peter 5:7).

I have noticed that women are generally more fearful and anxious than men. To the extent this is true, I believe the reason might relate to brain structure. A man's brain is geared to dealing with one thing at a time. A woman's brain, however, keeps several things in consciousness all the time, thus providing opportunity to be concerned with more than one thing at a time. Satan, of course, knows this and works hard to keep a woman upset through keeping her concerned and worried about many things.

6. *Rejection is another major reaction that has to be dealt with in deep-level healing.* And with rejection come abandonment and neglect. In these instances, the reaction is coming at us rather than from us. That is, the initial focus is on others rather than ourselves. We soon make it our reaction, however, by rejecting ourselves in response to perceived rejection by someone else.

The first signals I received from my mother while in her womb were of her rejection of a pregnancy that came too soon. I interpreted her rejection of the pregnancy as a rejection of me. Not knowing any better at the time, I assumed she was rejecting me because of some fault in myself, so I turned to rejecting myself. This was my habit for about the first fifty years of my life. I could not explain my success in life—success for which I felt totally unworthy—given my feeling that I did not deserve to be accepted by others or even by Jesus.

Many of my clients lost a parent through divorce or death early in life and fell into a lifelong pattern of expecting rejection from others, and therefore they rejected themselves. *If significant others reject or abandon me,* they reason, *I must be worthless and deserve to be rejected.*

Young children who lose a parent through death often do not realize that death was not the parent's choice. And they often reason that it is their fault if a parent leaves through death or divorce. Knowing they have been abandoned, they internalize the guilt.

Being neglected when we are young can have a similar effect. A child often feels neglected or abandoned when a sibling is born or when the family moves and he or she has to leave old friends and make new ones. Parents seldom completely understand the impact a move to another home, neighborhood and school has on their children.

Fortunately, however, the healing is usually great when an adult struggling with rejection goes back to these memories and experiences Jesus in them.

7. *Lust, often accompanied by pornography, is another major reaction we need to address, especially in men.* God gave males a very strong sex drive, and few of us are able to cope with it successfully by ourselves. Fortunately, we are promised that God will enable us to deal with it. Paul assured the Corinthians:

Every test that you have experienced is the kind that normally comes to people. But God keeps his promise, and he will not allow you to be tested beyond your power to remain firm; at the time you are put to the test, he will give you the strength to endure it, and so provide you with a way out.

1 Corinthians 10:13

Temptations abound, and even our spouses seldom understand what is going on and how to deal with it. Satan is quick to focus his activities here, feeding our feelings of shame and guilt and the anger and self-rejection resulting from failure in this area.

But Jesus is there: in the present, in the past, in the future. He experienced what we experience, tempted in all areas in which we are tempted, yet without sin (see Hebrews 4:15). And He is ready to enter our memories to heal the guilt and shame, ready to enter our present with us to enable us to put our sexuality into its proper place in our lives. This may be the hardest area for young men, especially if they try to fight the temptations alone. To gain the victory and freedom we seek in sexual areas, we first need to go back in our lives, with Jesus, to find any roots of brokenness and then move into the present with Him for help in keeping away from pornography, fantasy and other sexually stimulating activities.

8. *Though there are many more areas that could be dealt with, I will list just one more: pride.*

There are two kinds of pride. The good kind is sometimes called "ego strength." This is the ability to lift our heads high, knowing who we are and what God thinks of us.

The bad kind of pride is just the opposite; it shakes its fist in God's face and says, "I'll do things my way—I don't want You in my life." This kind of pride acts as if there is no accountability, no reckoning. We go through life trampling over other people to advance our own position, and when we get to the top we take all the credit for making it. The essence of this kind of pride is to claim that I have everything together and don't need any help, especially from God.

Pride is often a reaction to feelings of low self-worth. As we grow up we develop strategies to cover up our insecurities and feelings of unworthiness. Perhaps the most common strategy is to act as if we are confident when we are actually apprehensive, strong when we are actually weak, proud when we are actually fearful—all the while afraid that someone will see through our charade.

Sometimes God brings failure into our lives to call our bluff. And He is always there to pick us up if we will let Him. How much better it is, though, to start with the humility that recognizes that we are only here by God's permission, obeying the source of our life rather than exalting ourselves as if there is no accountability. In interacting with Jesus and following His example, then, we can humble ourselves under the mighty hand of God, and He will lift us up in His own good time (see 1 Peter 5:6).

So, whether the problems are spiritual or emotional, their ability to cripple, whether consciously or unconsciously, is great. And many are prisoners to such issues. I believe we are called as Christians to minister healing and freedom to the "captives" (see Luke 4:18–19), as Jesus did. That is what this book and the ministry it is intended to encourage is about. God has called us all to freedom: first to receive it ourselves, then to help others with the help He has brought to us. As the apostle Paul observed:

> [God] helps us in all our troubles, so that we are able to help others who have all kinds of troubles, using the same help that we ourselves have received from God.
>
> 2 Corinthians 1:4

3

How Things Are Stored: *Memories*

Steve was in deep difficulty. He wanted to be a good husband and father. But his frequent losing battle with his temper was doing him in. His wife, Mary, was now considering taking the children and going to live with her parents, at least till Steve got help. They were Christians—deeply committed to Christ—even hoping to serve as overseas missionaries. If only Steve could gain control of himself.

Neither Steve nor Mary had bargained for this kind of situation. Though they had both grown up in mildly dysfunctional homes, after coming to Christ they assumed that when they met the right marriage partner all would be well. Steve's frequent blowups, however, had burst that bubble and thrown their relationship into uncharted waters.

Their pastor had suggested that Steve find a Christian counselor to help him deal with his problem. Through this Steve found a measure of help. The counselor was able to help him relate his problem to the fact that during his growing-up years his father used outbursts of anger to get his way, especially when he had been drinking. Steve's mother simply put up with the tantrums, giving in to whatever his father wanted when he blew up.

Mary, however, was not as docile as Steve's mom. Her home had been calm, though filled with fear and distrust. When her father got angry, he exerted control in a different, quiet way. He did not get outwardly upset or loud—until that horrible day when he blew up and left the house and his family's lives. Mary had no practice dealing with overt expressions of anger. Afraid that Steve, like her father, would leave her and the children, Mary tended to dissolve in fear and mistrust when Steve blew up.

The counselor suggested that when Steve felt his anger building he stop, take a deep breath and pray. Occasionally Steve was able to do this. But when he got angry he usually found that he was unable to help himself or allow God to help him. And now, as the children were getting older and needing more discipline, Steve was losing control more often. In order to protect the children and herself, Mary was desperate and contemplating the unthinkable—leaving Steve.

Though this is not an actual story—Steve and Mary are typical, not actual characters—the problem is an actual problem that people go to counselors with day after day. Problems with anger are extremely common. So are problems with fear, self-rejection, shame and a host of other emotions that usually stem from childhood experiences and interfere with our adult lives, often controlling and sometimes crippling us.

Being a Christian Is Not Enough

When such problems become obvious we are often advised to go to a counselor, since they are thought to be good at analyzing such problems and helping us cope with them. But

I have had literally hundreds of clients tell me that, although they got help from professional counselors, especially if the counselor was a Christian, they did not get healed. They got analyzed but not fixed. As Christians, then, we ask, Where is healing? Where is the freedom Jesus promised us when He said, "If the Son sets you free, then you will be really free" (John 8:36)?

It is no secret that even Christians have emotional and spiritual problems. I often reflect on how so many believers have been blindsided by this fact. They are Christians. And usually they have worked hard at growing in their Christian experience. But they cannot seem to work through or out of their problems merely by doing the things Christians have to do to grow in their faith.

Frequently they are discouraged because a pastor misled them by citing Philippians 3:13–14, where the apostle Paul counsels us to forget those things that are behind us as we press forward toward the wonderful prize Jesus has for us in the future. But those who assume that Paul is counseling us simply to forget the bad things that have happened to us are misusing the passage. In its context we see that what Paul has in mind is that we are to put behind us the *good things*, the things in which we can take pride. Like a runner, we need to take our minds off the prizes we have won in the past if we are going to win the present race. If, in the middle of a race, we take our eyes off the finish line and stop to parade our past accomplishments, we will lose the race.

In actuality, research shows that even though we may try to forget bad experiences in the past, the pictures of those experiences remain in our memories and sabotage us when we least expect it.[1] Though we may bury the memory, our reaction to current events in our lives is often rooted in the way we reacted to the past event. The hurts are just too deep

55

for us simply to turn off the pain. We may stuff the memories and think they no longer affect us because the memories are not in the forefront of our thinking. But the memories lie there ready to ambush us when we least expect it, unconsciously pushing us to behave in embarrassing ways and leaving us to wonder what caused the reaction.

Such embarrassing behavior often seems to have nothing to do with what is presently going on in our lives. Though people like Steve learned to throw temper tantrums from a parent while they were growing up, as adults they find themselves unable to predict when such flare-ups will happen. Psychologists suggest that something in the present triggers a memory of something in the past, whereupon we react in some way reminiscent of our reaction to that past event.

Memories and Their Significance

Those who study memory have come up with several points of great relevance to our concern that people gain freedom from bondage to the past. My abstracting from their writings—especially Daniel Schacter's book *Searching for Memory* and Alan Baddeley's book *Your Memory*—yields the following list:

1. Many believe our brains start recording just about everything that happens to us by about six to eight weeks of gestation.[2]
2. We are told that we remember experiences in pictures, not in words. This is called *episodic* memory.
3. We are also told that we remember more of the bad things that happen to us than of the good things.
4. Further, our memory of the bad things is more vivid and more accurate than our memory of the good things that have happened to us.

5. Though our memories don't actually retain everything that happens to us, they retain a great deal.

6 What we call inability to remember is really *inability to recall*. The memories are usually there but we may not be able to bring them to consciousness.

7. What can be brought to consciousness and the accuracy of the memory are greatly affected by the strength of the impression an event has on us. The strength of the impression, then, may be determined to a large extent by the expectation with which we enter an event.

8. Contrary to popular belief, we do lose memories. Not everything that happens remains imprinted on our brains.

9. Memories are not always factual. Many memories have been affected by more recent events. And some memories are more like dreams than like records of facts.

10. The Holy Spirit can enable us to access memories we can't recall.

11. Memories stored in pictures can be healed only through picturing. Picture-memories cannot be healed through words alone, only through a healing picture.

12. The most effective healing memory is picturing the painful event with Jesus in it. Jesus is omnipresent, so we know He was there. So, when we picture the hurtful memory with Jesus in it, we are picturing the truth. He then heals from inside the memory.[3]

Such insights have enormous implications for our task of deep-level healing. For one thing, the fact that memory starts so early means we need to explore prebirth memories in our quest to discover the roots of current problems. And the fact that our minds record almost everything, whether or not we can recall things, means that if we can just access those memories and go back with Jesus to the memory roots of present-day actions and attitudes, we have a powerful tool to use to bring healing. In addition, the fact that we remember most clearly the bad things, the difficult times, the traumas, gives us quite an advantage in attempting to bring healing to past hurts.

The relationship between the strength of an impression and our ability to recall events, then, helps explain why some people can recall lots of things while others do not seem to recall very much at all.

Three Types of Long-Term Memory

In *Searching for Memory*, Daniel Schacter, chair of psychology at Harvard, speaks of short-term, or "working," memory and long-term memory. In dealing with emotional healing, it is usually long-term memory upon which we need to focus. Schacter points out that we have three types of long-term memory.

The first type, which he labels "procedural," is where we store what we need to know to operate our arms, legs, reflexes and the like. It is *procedural memory* that enables motor skills such as walking, driving a car and riding a bicycle and also emotional reflexes such as reacting to life experiences in anger, fear, shame, guilt and the like. It is the emotional reaction activity of this area of memory that is especially relevant in seeking to bring deep-level healing to people.

A second type of long-term memory is what Schacter calls *semantic memory*. This is our memory of facts, information and all other things that are word- and logic-based. The things we remember from schooling and from news broadcasts get stored in this part of our memory. From that storehouse we regularly bring up information needed to deal with whatever life brings our way. This is an important part of our memory and one that both schools and churches emphasize. But this is not where most people live.

It is the third type of memory that is most influential in our lives. This is what Schachter calls *episodic memory*. This part of memory is picture-based rather than word-based. This is where we remember feelings and emotions, relationships and personal experiences. This is where we live. And this is where we store our hurts. It is the place where wounds are stored and which needs to be accessed if we are to achieve spiritual and emotional healing. Therefore, this is the area of memory that is of most interest to us. Our techniques, then, need to be those that access this part of people's memories if we are to see them get well.[4]

Buried Memories

We have learned from psychologists that we regularly bury disagreeable feelings. This ability is often a good thing, as it enables us to survive rather than to fall apart in response to some pretty hurtful experiences. That survival, however, often comes at a price. For our reaction may not disappear once the abuse is over. Instead, the reaction gets stored along with the memory itself.

Our lives are like a deep well. As we look down into that well, we can see the surface clearly. But in order to get beneath the surface we have to find ways of accessing memory. This is where the Holy Spirit comes in: He is able to turn the water in our well on its side, allowing us to see and deal with memories that come from deep in that well—even things recorded in our brains that we cannot recall. Prebirth memories are there. Childhood memories are there also, even if we are unable to consciously recall them.

The Holy Spirit has access to the memories we cannot recall, even to the things we have worked hard to suppress, if we give Him permission. He may or may not bring the memories to our consciousness, but He can dig deep into our memory banks and bring deep healing.

To use another analogy, we may picture our memories as contained in capsules. Within each memory capsule, recorded in a picture, are the *facts* of an event plus the *feelings* we had during that event. Those capsules, then, are like the air-filled balls we take swimming with us. When we force such balls under water, it takes energy to keep them down. And sometimes the balls leak. This happens when we have experiences in the present that somehow remind us of earlier disagreeable experiences and trigger the reaction buried in the memory capsule to bob to the surface. This results in a reaction appropriate to the earlier experience rather than to the present experience. If the earlier experience was during childhood, I may react as a child would, even though I am an adult.

If we picture the "air" inside these capsules, or balls, as the feelings we are trying to keep submerged, we need to get to the contents of the capsules if we want to get healed. *We cannot change the facts, but with the Holy Spirit working inside of us we can change the feelings.* In order to deal with the feelings, however, we first need to open the capsules, allowing us to re-feel the feelings so that we can address them. We need to deal with them in the love and power of Jesus, recognizing the truth that Jesus was there and picturing Him in the memory, sharing the event with us and willingly taking upon Himself our past hurtful reaction. We will review this technique in more detail in chapter 5.

The Impact of Damaged Memories

We are told that even physical problems are rooted in emotional dysfunction. I have heard that as many as 80 percent of physical problems are estimated to have emotional—and, I would add, spiritual—roots. I have even heard that a medical doctor made the statement, "If people would learn to forgive, our hospitals would be empty." Given my experience that unforgiveness is the most important issue to be dealt with in deep-level healing, I would agree with that statement.

During a weekend seminar in which I was teaching and demonstrating deep-level healing, I was privileged to minister to three women, each of whom had a serious physical problem. Two had been in auto accidents about six months prior to the seminar, accidents that had left them with incapacitating back problems. The third had severely damaged one of her knees playing volleyball. Each had been greatly disappointed that, in spite of the time that had elapsed since the injuries, their bodies had not gotten well. Rather than focusing at first on their physical problems, I invited the Holy Spirit to take them back to prebirth, childhood and later memories. As He did this, in each case we came upon emotional damage that had likely weakened their bodies' natural physical healing mechanisms, thus denying them the recovery our bodies are intended to bring. The Holy Spirit then healed them from the damage of these earlier experiences, and in each case healed their physical problem as well.

Here is what I remember of the story one of these women told me. Carla twisted her knee badly while playing volleyball. She was taken to a doctor, who put her leg in a cast and gave her crutches to get around. She came to the seminar using the crutches. We sat down and, as is my habit, I began to ask questions about her life and her accident. Carla told me a number of things about herself that led me to believe she had a self-image problem. She also told me that when she returned to the doctor after two weeks he exclaimed that she was in worse shape than she had been immediately after the accident.

Now God designed us so that a healthy body begins repairing a problem immediately after it occurs. So Carla's condition should have improved during the two weeks between doctor visits. That her condition got worse rather than better alerted me to the fact that there was something in her system that was preventing her body from doing what it should about the injury. My guess, then, was that dealing with the emotional problems she had indicated would at the very least enable her body to deal more effectively with the physical problem.

So we began to deal with Carla's memories, starting with conception and working up through childhood, the process I describe in chapter 6 as "Two Hours to Freedom." As she encountered the presence of Jesus in each memory, and gave Him the hurts she felt from the various experiences of her life, Carla began to feel lighter and to accept and love herself. At one point I asked Jesus to show her the crown and gown she was entitled to wear as a princess in the Kingdom of God. That vision greatly helped her to move from self-hatred to loving and accepting herself as the person Jesus wanted her to be.

And, as usual, demons were there, enemy spirits that had attached themselves to Carla's negative attitudes toward herself. As she gave her hurts to Jesus and forgave those who had hurt her, the demons got weaker and were easy to kick out.

As we finished, after about an hour and a half, I asked Carla to check on her leg to see if there was any change. And indeed there was! She stood up and walked around without her crutches, without a limp and without pain! In the process of healing her internal attitudes, Jesus also healed her physical problem.

This is but one of hundreds of cases I have been involved with in which dealing with hurtful memories has resulted in both emotional and physical healing.

Jesus in the Memories

An important aim of counseling is to deal with the feelings (reactions) contained in the memory capsules. As mentioned, we cannot change the facts of what actually occurred, but under certain circumstances we can change the feelings accompanying the reaction. The main circumstance that results in healing is experiencing Jesus in the memories. He is omnipresent, so we know He was there when the events recorded in our memories occurred. Experiencing Him in the memories, then, is experiencing the truth. This is not New Age guided imagery, where a person imagines something he or she would like to have happen—attempting, by doing so, to construct a different reality. This is experiencing the truth that Jesus was present in the actual events of the past.

As we experience Jesus' presence, then, we can give to Him the crippling reactions stored in our memories and avail ourselves of His desire and power to heal. Our submerged memories, especially of the bad things that have happened to us, are very alive inside us, available to be accessed and able to be healed under the guidance and power of Jesus. Professional counselors have learned to access such memories. But since they typically do not invite the presence of Jesus into those memories, they usually are limited in their ability to help their clients get fully healed. They depend on only the human power the client is able to command. This human power can help but is not likely to bring complete healing. Working in Jesus' power, however, makes healing the usual result.

In professional counseling the feeling may be identified, but there is seldom sufficient power to enable the counselee to change that feeling and to "heal" the memory. This is why we need the power of Jesus to empower the counseling techniques we employ.

"Was Jesus there when the abuse happened?" I asked Becky.

I have asked this question hundreds of times. It had never occurred to Becky that Jesus had been present during the abuse. It felt like she had been abandoned by her Savior. She had been taught that Jesus could do anything at any time, so she was angry at Him for not preventing the abuse. She had never learned that when God gave humans free will He was placing certain limits on Himself—limitations that meant that Jesus could not keep the man who had abused her from using his free will to hurt her.

Becky knew in her mind that Jesus is omnipresent. So she reasoned that He must have been there when the abuse happened.

"Would you like to see Jesus in your memory?" I asked. "Would you like me to ask the Holy Spirit to let you see what He was doing?" I further explained that when we see Jesus in such memories we are not just imagining something that did not really happen. No, we are picturing the truth. Jesus really was there, even though we were not aware of His presence when the event happened. The Holy Spirit enables us to experience this truth when we ask Him.

God, in Jesus, has promised, "I will never leave you; I will never abandon you" (Hebrews 13:5). He is there when things go right. He is there when things go wrong. And most people, under the guidance of the Holy Spirit, can picture this truth in their memories. Becky closed her eyes and went back to the memory. Almost immediately she saw Jesus standing there.

"What is He doing?" I asked.

"He's crying," she replied, "and it looks as though He's about to pull my uncle off my twelve-year-old inner child. But now my uncle is finished and gets off her himself, and Jesus moves in and holds her. She's crying, but Jesus is comforting her."

"Can you help your twelve-year-old inner self give Jesus her shame, her pain and her anger?" I asked.

"Yes, she's giving Him those things."

"How about forgiveness? Can she give your uncle to Jesus? He's promised, 'I will take revenge, I will pay back' (see Romans 12:19). Can your twelve-year-old inner self trust Jesus to keep His promise and do what she cannot do—pay her uncle back?"

"Yes, she can."

When I first began to ask people to invite Jesus into such events, I was a bit fearful that they would get even more angry with Jesus because He did not stop the abuse. But this has happened only once or twice during 25 years of doing inner healing ministry. With those couple of exceptions, abuse victims have felt accepted and comforted in the memory rather than angry at Jesus, especially when I could truthfully tell that younger part of the person that her future would be better— the abuse would stop—and that Jesus was there, protecting her from the abuse being even worse than it was.

One problem people have is that they expect Jesus, in light of all His power, to prevent bad experiences such as sexual abuse. Though He does protect us from many such experiences, He does not promise to keep us from all such experiences—only to be with us in them. Unfortunately, He allows even committed Christians to have accidents and to undergo tangles with abuse and other evils. However, when He says, "I will never abandon you," He means just that. He is there, He cares and He participates in every aspect of our lives, good or bad. This participation, though, is not visible in our memories until the Holy Spirit enables us to see and/or feel it.

Christ was indeed there when Becky was being hurt, and He was on Becky's side. He participated in her shame. And the perpetrator will have to pay for it when Jesus starts paying people back for what they have done. But for now He simply wants us to give Him the burden that such misuse leaves us with so that we can be free of the crippling effects of shame, hatred, anger, fear or other legitimate feelings. And when we give Him these feelings, we get to go free.

During these ministry sessions, Jesus allows us to feel and usually to see His presence in the memory of the event. We can then respond to His invitation to "Come to me, all of you who are tired from carrying heavy loads, and I will give you rest" (Matthew 11:28). As we come to Him, then, accepting His invitation to exchange our hurts and hurtful attitudes for His peace, we get healed from the inside stuff that has kept us captive. Jesus heals our reactions as well as the wounds, changing the wounds to scars—scars that don't hurt.

In ministry situations, the Holy Spirit guides us as we look at one memory after another. I invite the client to picture each memory with Jesus in it, thus enabling the person to experience a truth he or she was not aware of before and then to experience the freedom Jesus provides to those who give their heavy loads to Him. The memories may come one by one or in bunches, and may be healed one by one or by type. That is, dealing with a given type of memory may result in the healing of many memories of that same type.

What about False Memories?

Several years ago there was quite a fuss about the possibility that certain counselors might be feeding false memories to their clients. In counseling situations, the counselor is in a position of power and could suggest things that vulnerable individuals might take to an extreme. So it is always possible that certain irresponsible counselors might try to implant false memories in people's minds. The opportunity is there, and our ability to check up on such activity is pretty limited.

So what do we do?

We do need to recognize that this could be a problem and that our search for memories can sometimes lead to supposed memories that are in fact false. This being the case, do we turn away from seeking to get at roots through dealing with memories? Or is there some way to make sure the memories are accurate?

These are legitimate questions, but I think they are the wrong ones to ask. I believe the right question is, Did anything significant happen, especially anything negative? If there is a feeling that something happened or a memory of something, we need to get at dealing with it. But by "dealing with it," I mean we want the person to confront the possibility that something is there that Jesus wants to heal. And the healing will come through first inviting Jesus into whatever the event might be. Secondly, then, we give the event and all its pain to Jesus and forgive the perpetrator.

However unclear we might be as to what really happened, the aim is to give both the event, including any person(s) involved, and all ensuing negative reactions to Jesus. Thus, the accuracy of the memory is not the major issue. Giving the feelings to Jesus, letting Him take away the damaged emotions, is the important thing.

The memory experts tell us that memories are often less than totally factual. They may be more like dreams than news reports, with the details remembered symbolically rather than factually. And early memories are often "contaminated" with later understandings and attitudes. An inner child memory, for example, often involves the child thinking or speaking at a more advanced level than he or she would have been able to do during the actual event.

67

So if there is pain or discomfort in a memory, we need to deal with it. But *the issue is dealing with the pain or discomfort and getting the person healed, not working hard to learn exactly what happened.* Knowing the details accurately is seldom necessary for healing. Forgiveness and giving our feelings to Jesus, however, are always necessary.

If the memory in fact happens to be false raises an interesting concern. We might in reality have led a person to forgive someone who did not do anything wrong. My response would be, "No problem." If that is the case, we simply have wasted a bit of time. Far worse would be not to forgive someone who *has* done something wrong.

So I am not worried at all about the possibility of false memories—except in one area. I know of a couple who entered professional counseling and were led to see the negative effects of their upbringings and then advised to seek healing through confronting their parents with all the things they had done wrong. So they confronted their parents, destroying their relationship with them over issues that could not be rectified, and in the process they severely damaged both their parents and themselves.

This is wrong! If their parents made mistakes—and they did—the important thing is not the mistakes but forgiveness. It is possible that telling their parents off made the children feel a bit better, but it did not heal them or their parents. Only facing the facts realistically, including the fact that the mistakes could not be undone, and forgiving the parents for what they had done could heal them. Creating new wounds while not adequately dealing with the old ones never brings healing. These two people tried to get healed by damaging relationships that did not need to be damaged. I am not sure that either they or their parents ever completely recovered from this ill-advised attempt at healing.

Repression of Memories

People usually do not like to keep negative memories in their consciousness. Therefore they repress or suppress them. Such memories are like open wounds; they fester inside of us like physical wounds that have been bandaged but not treated with antiseptic. And the infection often gets worse as time passes.

Repressing memories never gets them healed. Healing can come only by facing the memories with Jesus. Jesus' way of dealing both with sin and with wounds is to face them squarely and to work straight through them. If we ignore or repress either sin or emotional wounds, they never get healed.

Satan, of course, is very active in keeping us from facing negative past memories. He controls many people through their fear of the past. He does not want anyone to face the painful truth and to apply Jesus' healing power. Experiencing Jesus' presence in the memories, then, is like the medicine we put on physical wounds.

Reliving past memories, however, may be painful. Dealing with past hurts is "emotional surgery." Just as physical surgery is painful, so is emotional surgery. The pain of surgery, though, because of the expectation of health and freedom from pain afterward, is quite different from the pain of an unhealed open wound or a broken bone.

Infected Wounds

Physical wounds, if not treated, become infected. Emotional wounds, if not cared for, likewise get worse. We may ignore them, repress them or try to forget them; but they lie there just the same, causing disruption from inside. They often function from beneath our consciousness, though occasionally we may realize we have reacted in a way that goes beyond what an occasion warrants. As David Seamands has pointed out, "Whenever you experience a response on your part that is way out of proportion to the stimulus, then look out. You have probably tapped into some deeply hidden emotional hurt."[5]

When I speak at seminars I like to ask how many in the audience, since they have been adults, ever have acted like children. Usually almost every person raises his or her hand. I take it, then, that nearly all of us experience reactions buried deep beneath the surface that bob up from time to time, alerting us to the fact that something within us has not yet been resolved.

The memories are there, holding both good and bad stuff. We need to get at the bad memories in order to get them healed. I have found that the easiest way to access these memories is by finding them in the parts of us in which they are stored. We can do so by contacting the inner parts that I call "inner children" or "inner adults." To this subject we now turn.

4

Our Inner Selves

The reason Amelia came to me was because she was losing her temper when she disciplined her children. She would go too far, she told me, and then feel tremendous guilt because she knew they did not deserve the severity of the discipline. Nevertheless, time after time she found it impossible to control herself.

In accordance with my usual practice, I asked the Holy Spirit to take Amelia back to the memories stored in her brain during the months before birth while she was being carried in her mother's womb. I often find that the roots of a person's presenting problem are stored in his or her prebirth memories. Amelia was not wanted by her parents when she was conceived. Since they were extremely poor and struggling to support the two children they already had, the last thing they needed was another pregnancy.

As we went through the months of gestation in our exercise, Amelia experienced what appeared to be an attempt by her mother to abort her. (The reality of this event was later confirmed by her mother.) As we focused on the third month of gestation, Amelia started shaking and saying repeatedly, "Poking, poking, poking." Her reaction to the attempted abortion produced part of the "garbage" we needed to deal with to get her healed. For all of her 35 years, Amelia had carried a deep-seated anger toward her parents without knowing why. But something within her remembered and, prodded by the Holy Spirit, revealed the roots of her anger.

We also had to deal with the guilt Amelia experienced over the way she treated her children. This guilt formed another part of her emotional garbage, as did the deeply felt shame she experienced and tried to hide coming from the fact that she was not wanted when she was conceived and born. The guilt and shame set Amelia up to believe a series of lies from the evil one concerning who she was and whether she even had a right to exist. Her self-image, consequently, was extremely low, and she found no way to square her negative feelings toward herself with what she knew in her mind concerning the value Jesus put on her.

In addition, in keeping with the tradition of her Chinese society, Amelia had been dedicated at birth to the gods of her family, creating spiritual garbage to add to her emotional garbage. Then she had to deal with a series of unpleasant life experiences with her parents, teachers, classmates, romantic partners, work associates, husband, mother-in-law, children and others. Amelia had not been physically or sexually abused, but we uncovered several experiences that had created emotional wounds that had never healed. In short, she was full of emotional and spiritual garbage that cried out for deep-level healing.

The good news is that God, in His grace, healed Amelia, freeing her from this longstanding spiritual and emotional bondage. She was then free to treat her children fairly and to love herself as she knew in her mind that Jesus loved her.

Unwantedness

A fairly common type of problem having its roots in prebirth experience is the negative self-image that many struggle with stemming from the fact that their parents did not want them at conception. Many of us fall into this category. Perhaps our parents were not married, or a pregnancy may have been inconvenient at the time or they wanted a child of the opposite sex. There are many reasons why parents may not want a child. Unfortunately, that feeling is communicated to the infant in the womb, creating a wound that leads the child to feeling guilty about living. This often is the root of feelings such as shame, self-rejection, low self-esteem, unworthiness and inadequacy.

I once ministered to a pastor's wife who hated herself but could not understand why. Andrea told me she felt she was "just taking up space that really belonged to someone else"! She played the organ in their church but was so ashamed of herself that she could never bring herself to walk down the center aisle of the church to get to the organ if anyone was sitting in the pews. She would always slink down the side aisle, play the organ and, at the end of the service, slink back up that aisle to get out of the church, hopefully without anyone noticing her.

Andrea could not put her finger on the roots of her self-hatred until we began to examine the way she had been treated by her parents. They had not planned on her and did not value her. This unwantedness, implanted in Andrea's memory long before birth, was very alive in influencing her current attitudes and behavior, though deeply hidden in her subconscious. Although she recognized, with the help of a psychologist, her surface-level self-hatred, she knew of no way to get at it and get it healed.

In our ministry session, we asked Jesus to go back with Andrea into her prebirth memories, making His presence known and blessing the memory of each month. As she experienced Jesus in the memory of each month of gestation, she began to feel a lightness, as if a heavy load was being lifted off her shoulders. This feeling continued and grew as Andrea pictured Jesus holding her at birth and especially as she pictured her adult self holding the newborn baby self. We then continued picturing Jesus in the memories of her childhood, teenage years and on into her adult life.

As Andrea remembered the various events of her life and experienced the presence of Jesus in each memory, she was able to give Him the pain she felt in each situation. As we went through this typical deep-level healing process, in the love and power of Jesus, she came to understand and accept in the deepest parts of her the fact that she was planned and chosen by Jesus, as God, even before the creation of the world (see Ephesians 1:4). By experiencing Jesus' presence in these early memories, Andrea came to understand that she was wanted by Jesus and, though an accident to her parents, was no accident to Him. Therefore, she got to choose whether to continue to allow her parents' attitude to govern her life or to agree with Jesus in valuing her life as He valued her. When she chose to accept Jesus' attitude toward her, Andrea's life was radically changed.

I will describe this process more fully in the pages to come. Suffice it to say here that when people experience Jesus in the memories of past events, wonderful things usually happen. Since He is omnipresent, we know that He was there. So I am not simply guiding my clients into an imagined imagery; they are picturing truth—truth that they have not seen before, experiential truth that brings healing.

Wounds

There are many sources of wounds in addition to unwantedness. A child may develop a physical problem and be forced to spend time in a hospital, away from parental nurturing. This can create feelings of abandonment and fear, wounds stemming from the child's inability to understand what is happening. Or verbal, physical or sexual abuse may wound children and cause them to turn in on themselves. Such treatment communicates to them that they are worthless and often pushes them to strive to perform at a high level in order to win the approval of parents and/or other significant people in their lives.

We are thus wounded in many ways as children and usually blame ourselves for our problems. Whether in the womb or in early childhood, we do not understand that grownups have problems and that the way they feel toward us or treat us stems from *their* problems, not *ours*. Therefore, if we are mistreated we assume it is our own fault and turn against ourselves.

I grew up feeling that my father did not like me. So, assuming that the reason I felt unloved and unwanted was my own fault, I hated myself. I tried and tried to do things that would win my father's approval, but long after I had succeeded I still felt I had not made it. I felt all my achievements were a mistake.

Then, when I was about fifty years old, my wife figured out that my parents were not married at the time I was conceived. Knowing what I do now about the influences of a mother's feelings on a preborn child, I could understand the roots of my self-hatred and invite that preborn part of me to understand and forgive. This, then, freed me to learn to love myself.

Perhaps this raises the question, "Can people, using these techniques, bring themselves healing without the assistance of others?" The answer is that it is possible, and many do bring about partial or complete healing by working alone (with Jesus) or with someone who is not an "expert." My favorite example of this is a woman who called me after reading one of my books. She had realized that she would likely never be able to meet with me for ministry, since she lived in

Baltimore and I lived in California. So she ordered another copy of the book for a friend. She then gave the book to her friend, asking her to follow the book and get her healed. Her friend, she reported, with the book as her guide but with no previous experience, ministered to her and got her free. Then they changed places and her friend also got healed!

When we access memories by going back to them and experiencing Jesus in them (either with help or alone), we face the wounds and work straight through them rather than trying to ignore them. Memories of wounds are very much alive inside us, whether or not we realize the fact. And these memories can be accessed and healed with Jesus' help. As they are healed, Jesus changes the wounds to scars. We still can recognize the scars and remember the hurts. But scars, though they are reminders, do not hurt.

People Have "Parts"

We all have identifiable inner entities that may be called "inner parts." When we talk to ourselves, it is as if one part of us is talking to another part. When we adopt a different behavior in one situation than in another, it is as if we take on a different persona or role. It seems as though we can be quite a different person in one situation than in another.

And this is often a good thing. For example, my grandchildren probably would find it difficult to relate to me if I behaved with them like I behave with the graduate students I teach at Fuller Seminary. In fact, these two roles in my life are so distinct that neither my grandchildren nor my students have much of an idea how I behave in the other relationship. On occasions when my students have visited our home when we are having a family party, they often have remarked that I am a completely different person in that context than I am in the classroom.

When it comes to different roles that we play, many of us have parts that may be labeled a "Poor little me" part or a "Listen to me—I'm in charge" part. Or we may have an "I'm a failure" part or an "I'll never get it right" part. Or many people have a part that says, "Fake it—put on a happy face even though you don't really feel that way." Many have a sexy part or a lustful part or a little boy or little girl part. Or a silent sufferer part or a complainer part or a "You've hurt me and I'm going to get even" part. Or the Charlie Brown part that says, "Normalcy for me is for things to go wrong, so if anything goes right it's a mistake."

Personally, though I have identified several of these parts in my life, the one that governed my life for many years was the part that kept saying, "You've got to make the team or excel in your studies or career to prove yourself to your father."

The parts that concern us here are those that are often called "inner children" or "inner adults." These are the parts that go by age and hold significant memories from years past. These are the parts that take over when certain memories are triggered by events in the present. They are often little boy parts or little girl parts, hence the name "inner children." But they may represent adult years as well, and thus may be labeled "inner adults."

A good example of this comes from my ministry time with Jim. I asked the Holy Spirit to help him picture himself as a little boy in his home. Jim saw himself at about age three or four, sitting on the living room floor and crying because his mother had gone out the door and left him all alone. His mother had said she would be right back. But what seemed to little Jim to be a long time had passed and she had not returned, leaving him with the fear that she would not be coming back.

So in his visualization Jim sat there crying, feeling a deep sense of abandonment and rejection. Though his mother returned in what to an adult was a short time, he was left with a sense of abandonment and rejection that constantly interfered with his adult life, including his relationships with his wife, his family and those with whom he worked.

Jim thought he long since had forgotten this memory, but in actuality he had repressed it because it was so painful. And that part of him that held the memory did not seem to know that his mother had come back. Instead, this three-year-old or four-year-old part of him seemed to hold on to the feelings of abandonment as if his mother's leaving was permanent and predicted similar abandonment and rejection whenever a significant person left him alone.

To bring healing to this younger part of Jim, I guided him in a way I have found to be very healing. First, I asked Jim for permission to talk to this three-year-old or four-year-old part of him that he was seeing in his memory. This granted, I asked Jim's younger part to look for Jesus in the event, explaining that since Jesus is omnipresent He must have been there even though the little boy was not aware of His presence at the time. Right away the Holy Spirit brought to little Jim a picture of Jesus standing nearby as he was crying. So I asked the little boy if he would like a hug from Jesus, and he said yes. Immediately Jim saw a picture of Jesus hugging his inner child, and the child, feeling comforted, stopped crying.

I then spoke to this very young part of Jim to let him know that his mother did, in fact, come right back and that he could give his fear and confusion to Jesus. The memory of his mother's return apparently had not registered in the same way as the memory of her leaving. But as Jim pictured Jesus there and hugging him, he was able to give his feelings of abandonment to Jesus and forgive his mother for leaving him.

The result was healing from a long-term problem. The process was to identify the younger part of Jim that was holding the feelings of abandonment and to help that part of him deal with those feelings by recognizing them and then forgiving his mother and giving the feelings to Jesus.

I have participated in hundreds of healings that have followed this pattern. By assuming that the root issue is held in a memory and accessing it through an inner child approach, I have seen person after person healed at the deepest level.

Memories seem to be held within what we might picture as capsules in two separable parts: the *fact* of the event that is remembered, plus the *feelings* that were generated during that event. For little Jim, the fact was that his mother did leave him alone. There was, however, another fact—one that little Jim was quite unaware of when he was crying—that Jesus was there with him, even before he had given his life to Jesus. We wanted little Jim to become conscious of this fact and to give Jesus his hurt, thus changing the feelings associated with the memory.

The Concept

So we all have identifiable inner entities that we can call "parts" or "sub-personalities." Though these can be identified in various ways, our concern here is for the parts we call "inner children" or "inner adults." These are the result of a mild form of dissociation that people create quite normally, often (though not exclusively) at times when there is some kind of difficult experience.

Most people, with little difficulty, can close their eyes and "see" one or more objectified inner selves. These inner selves hold memories of events that happened at the age they represent. Since Jesus is omnipresent, we know He was there when these events happened. So I can invite my clients to picture Him in their memories, knowing that when they do so they are picturing the truth. We are not asking them to go on flights of fancy through a New Age type of guided imagery. Jesus was actually there in the event, even though the client was not conscious of that fact and may not have had a relationship with Jesus at the time.

Lucy shared with me that her father regularly beat her, often without her even knowing why. So I asked her to go back in her memory to a time when her father was beating her. Lucy saw herself as a teenager, curled up in a corner while her father wielded a stick; and she allowed herself to feel the emotions of that awful scene. I asked her, then, if she could see Jesus in her memory. She hesitated, and then reported, through her tears, that she did indeed see Him—down on the floor with her, joining her in taking her father's wrath. The fact that Jesus was sharing the experience with her made it possible for Lucy to turn her pain over to Him and, with a bit more encouragement, forgive her father.

Experiencing Jesus' presence in remembered negative events usually enables a person to give Him the negative feelings generated during the event. When the individual is able to give Jesus the anger, shame and other damaging emotions he or she is feeling, He is able to bring healing from the negative effects rooted in those feelings. And the person is then free to forgive the perpetrator as Jesus has commanded (see Matthew 6:14–15).

Again, people cannot change the facts of the events in which they were hurt; but they can, with Jesus' help, change the feelings generated in reaction to what happened. The hurts of negative events tend to be stored in our memories like open wounds. By experiencing Jesus in the events and giving Him our hurts, Jesus heals the wounds, leaving only scars that no longer hurt, though they may remind us of a time when the pain was great.

Are Inner Children Real?

Not everyone is convinced that "inner children," as we are calling them, actually exist. They claim that we are simply playing tricks on ourselves through manipulating our imaginations. To the doubters, I say, "Try it." The results usually make believers out of the skeptics.

Frankly, I do not know exactly what is happening. What I do know is that when I invite people to picture themselves at younger ages, they usually can do so. And when I ask people to treat that pictured part as a separate person, they usually can do so, even to the extent of seeing themselves hugging the inner person and carrying on a conversation with him or her. In fact, I, an outsider, can usually carry on a conversation with that inner part as well. And when I ask people how interacting with this inner person feels, they report that it is like interacting with a completely separate person. Or, even more interesting, many say something like, "I *was* fifteen (or four or ten or seventeen) again. I was no longer an adult. My words, my feelings, my attitudes, were those of my younger self."

For most people, then, the inner person is quite real, and the interaction is also real. It is as if there are other people inhabiting the individual's body, just waiting to be contacted and ready to deal with memories long suppressed. And when these memories are dealt with in the presence of Jesus, the roots of present-day problems are usually accessed, exposed and healed.

Some may object that I am simply inviting people to use their imaginations. There is some truth in that suggestion. However, there is a great difference between imagination guided simply by ourselves and imagination guided by the Holy Spirit. I believe that when we ask the Holy Spirit to guide us, it is He who works to guide our imaginations and our interactions with what we are calling our inner children. Holy Spirit–guided imagination is used greatly by God to bring healing of deep-level problems.

Of the many experiences I have had in interacting with inner selves, three stand out.

Heather

During a break at a seminar, Heather approached me and announced, "I've just met my fourteen-year-old inner child, and I *hate* her!"

"And how does she feel?" I asked.

"She hates me, too!"

Heather's teenage years had been rocky and filled with shame. Her way of coping with these embarrassing memories was to suppress both the memories and the feelings they generated within her. So Heather's fourteen-year-old part, one of the parts that was holding on to the memories, developed feelings of neglect, anger and hatred toward her adult parts.

My job was to help the two parts to forgive, accept and love each other. The first step, then, was to get adult Heather to promise forgiveness and acceptance of that part of her of which she was so ashamed. She agreed, speaking forgiveness to fourteen-year-old Heather. This led to the fourteen-year-old part opening herself to understanding that the adult did not know she was there and did not understand that suppressing the memories was doing damage to this part of her. This led to forgiveness and reconciliation, with the mutual hatred replaced by acceptance and love and sealed with a hug in Heather's visualization.

Heather left with these words, "I can't wait to meet my fifteen-year-old!"

Joyce

A second experience began with a telephone call from Joyce, with whom I had been working for several weeks. Joyce's problem was that whenever she tried to make contact with her thirteen-year-old inner child on her own (as I had taught her), she would see her younger part run away without speaking to her. Given Joyce's history of severe abuse, I suspected that this teenage part was hiding some major situation of abuse. When Joyce came for her next appointment, I asked the thirteen-year-old if I could talk to her. She reluctantly agreed; and then I asked if she would meet with adult Joyce if Jesus was present. Again, she agreed reluctantly.

I then spoke to adult Joyce, asking her to agree not to condemn but rather to accept and love her thirteen-year-old self no matter what she had to say. Adult Joyce agreed, and their meeting in Jesus' presence went well. The thirteen-year-old was indeed hiding an abusive experience, which she shared. And adult Joyce kept her promise to accept the inner self and to help her give her anger and shame to Jesus. This was followed, in Joyce's picturing, by both Jesus and adult Joyce hugging the inner child. Adult Joyce and her teenage inner self then got to be good friends in freedom.

April

While I was leading April, who was twenty-six years old, from one inner child to the next, we came across a very hurting fifteen-year-old. Though adult April had not intended to reveal it, her fifteen-year-old part blurted out that she had been raped! And, like many rape victims, she blamed herself for what had been done to her. This self-blame, then, fit into a pattern of self-hatred that pervaded her whole life.

April had been conceived before her parents were married. This fact provided the foundation for her self-hatred and also for her reaction to the rape. I knew this about her when I asked if I could speak to her fifteen-year-old. So I wanted to let that teenage part of her express herself fully in order to get out in the open the facts and the feelings, including both the forgiveness issues and the self-image issues. She cried as she recounted the rape event she had been hiding and the pain she had been living with for eleven years.

The fifteen-year-old part of April had to forgive the perpetrator, so I addressed this issue first. From her perspective, however, what he had done was secondary compared to her felt need to blame herself. So I reasoned with April's fifteen-year-old that the rape was really the man's problem, not hers. He was the one who had initiated the rape, and he is the one who will have to face Jesus someday concerning what he had done to an unwilling young woman. My argument was accepted, and fifteen-year-old April was able to give the perpetrator to Jesus and then forgive herself for any part she may have had in the event. She also had to forgive herself for holding on to the anger, shame and fear rooted in the rape experience.

All of this was done in interaction with the very much alive fifteen-year-old part of April, for it was that part that was hanging on to the destructive emotions and the self-hatred that her child parts (including her preborn parts) had already worked through and released. And it was that part that got free when she finally gave to Jesus her right to anger and hatred. It was the fifteen-year-old part of April that forgave, not the adult part who had long since forgiven the man.

Levels of Forgiveness

Many people are in this kind of situation, where the adult part of them has forgiven but some younger part(s) still holds the pain and unforgiveness resulting from an earlier experience. The younger parts of a person who has been hurt are usually very much alive within that person and needing the special kind of attention this inner child approach produces. Since forgiveness is such an important issue, this approach enables a person to forgive at the deepest levels.

People often have remarked that their sincerest attempts to forgive as adults did not feel complete until their younger inner selves forgave. This discovery was startling to me. I had never thought of levels of forgiveness, but apparently this is the case. That is, forgiving at the adult level is one thing; but forgiving at the deeper level, the level where the abuse happened, is quite another thing. If the abuse happened at age five, it is that part of the person—the five-year-old inner child—that needs to forgive the perpetrator in order for the person to get truly free.

Thus, forgiveness is an important issue for each inner self, as well as for the adult person.

Characteristics of Inner Children

What I am calling "inner children" or "inner persons" or "inner selves" is really a personification of memories. We recognize that memories of events are stored in our minds in pictures, with times attached to them. These events and times are retrievable, then, at various ages by addressing a person's inner selves, as I did in the previous examples.

Inner selves, even within the same person, may differ in "substance." That is, some inner selves seem as real as the person him- or herself, while others are quite vague. The fifteen-year-old April, for instance, was very substantial. Those who had known April at age fifteen testified that the voice, vocabulary and attitude were those of April when she was fifteen, not those of her adult twenty-six-year-old self.

85

Though we can talk to the inner self, there is often little or no verbal response. And the adult may "feel" the inner person more than see or hear him or her. We can speak, then, of weaker or stronger inner selves.

When searching for inner selves, the adult can usually tell from the inner person's posture how that part is feeling. The child often will appear in the adult's picture as angry or sad or lonely or showing some other negative emotion. On occasion the inner self will show anger at the adult, accusing him or her of neglect. I have heard angry inner children plead such things as "Why hasn't she paid attention to me? She knew I was here. I did many things to alert her to my presence." Whatever the feelings and whatever the source, though, it is healing for the inner person to experience Jesus as near and loving. His hugs, which the inner child pictures, take the person from captivity to freedom.

The adult also may find the inner self in a particular place, suggesting that the focus needs to be on the experience that happened in that place. The adult, for example, might see herself in a bedroom experiencing sexual abuse. Or the inner person might be seen lost in a store while his mother is shopping, or being criticized by a teacher in school, or hiding from an angry parent in a closet or being beaten up by a classmate on the school playground. The adult may see the inner child anywhere life happens. When the adult sees Jesus with the inner self in that place, though, is when healing happens.

What we are referring to here is mild dissociation. Though not a matter of multiple personalities, it is similar in many ways, and is most likely a weak form of multiple personality disorder (MPD).[1] Unlike MPD, however, a person's ability to find several inner selves is quite normal. Under extreme pressure, such as early childhood sexual abuse, inner children can become multiple personalities.

As I mentioned earlier, most adults can point to times when they acted or reacted like children. These times are commonly regarded as occasions in which an early memory is "triggered," releasing an emotion that was appropriate for the original experience but probably not for the present event. Such events can be seen as occasions when an inner child takes over, either briefly or for longer periods of time. This can be very embarrassing, of course, and the adult's reaction may be "Where did that come from?"

Finding and working with the inner selves, in conjunction with Jesus, brings healing from the reactions to the original events and results in freedom from such intrusions of memories in adult life. The usual result is that takeover episodes cease as damaged emotions from early in life get healed.

Ministry using the inner child technique can be done individually or in groups. I ask the Holy Spirit to bring up any inner children, especially hurting ones, and I ask the person for permission to talk with the inner children. I then interact with these inner selves, discovering what experiences need to be dealt with, and invite Jesus into these memories. I treat the inner self as a separate person and enable that inner person to find and give his or her problems to Jesus and to receive hugs from Jesus and from the adult person. I want positive relationships to develop between the inner person and Jesus and between that inner person and the adult.

When, as usual, someone needs to be forgiven, I help the inner child to forgive at the time (in memory) that the abuse happened. Again, this brings a deeper level of forgiveness than is possible when only the adult forgives.

So I find working with a person's inner selves to be the most effective way of getting at deep-level issues. Bringing Jesus into a relationship with these inner selves, then, usually brings the healing so badly needed by most people.

How to Use the Inner Child Technique

This approach can be used either in a "hit or miss" sort of fashion or in a more systematic way. The hit or miss usage can be very effective if the ministry leader is listening to the Holy Spirit while asking Him to take the client to whatever age(s) necessary in order to deal with critical issues. For example, if a person was sexually violated at age eight and is extremely upset about it, the Holy Spirit might well lead a ministry leader to deal with that first. Success with the event at age eight, then, might make it easier to deal with problems at other ages.

Alternatively, a leader might choose to start at conception and look for inner children year by year, dealing with whatever comes as they go through the ages. Anything that happened in each year is thus dealt with in sequence. I usually prefer to work this way unless I feel there are hindrances at younger ages because of the fact that we have not dealt with a significant event that took place later in the person's life.

Typically there are not inner children at every age. If abuse occurred at a given age, there likely will be an inner child at that age. If nothing noteworthy happened in a given year, there may not be an inner child. If more than one traumatic event happened in a given year, however, there may be more than one inner child for that year.

When inner selves get free, the client may see them playing or dancing with Jesus or doing some other pleasant activity. The objective is to see all the inner selves happy.

Once the inner healing is finished, we need to check to see if any demons have been attached to the problems we have just addressed.

5

Demonization

At the end of a class session in our healing course at Fuller, the speaker, as usual, invited the participants to receive ministry. Several of us formed groups to pray for people with various physical and emotional problems. I had just finished praying with someone when two of the women in the class asked me to help them pray for a woman who was acting strangely.

Several students had gathered around Mary and were praying for her. Leaning back stiffly against her chair, Mary's eyes were closed and she had an uncooperative look on her face. I was in the early days of learning to do inner healing and had not, as yet, confronted any demons. I remember saying to myself, though, *This is probably demons!*

I had learned that demons have to have a "legal right" to live inside people, so I challenged the demons in the name of Jesus Christ and commanded them to tell me what right they had to be there. Though it took a few minutes to get them to answer, they finally spoke through Mary, revealing that the grip they had on her was legitimate as long as she was unwilling to forgive several people.

Once we discovered the demons' legal right and led Mary to forgive those who had hurt her, the strength of the demons lessened noticeably and we were able to cast them out fairly easily—easily for us, that is. It was not easy for Mary to do the hard work of forgiving. In fact, she remarked afterward that she felt as though she had gone through major surgery. My response was, "You have. Inner healing is major emotional surgery."

In this case and in hundreds of others in which I have been involved over the past 25 years, it became clear that the strength of the demons—and indeed their ability to be there at all—derived from the person's disobedience to God's rules. Mary's problem was that she needed to forgive several people who had hurt her and against whom she was holding a grudge. Her unforgiveness not only was breaking one of God's most important rules but was providing "garbage" to which demonic "rats" had a right to attach themselves.

This chapter, then, introduces us to the presence and activities of demons in keeping us from experiencing all the freedom God has for us.

Demons Must Have "Legal Rights"

As we have seen in Mary's case, hanging on to unforgiveness gives the enemy a legal right to live in a person. While Jesus was on earth, forgiveness was one of His major themes. He commands us to forgive those who have hurt us in response to the forgiveness we have received from God. When we pray the Lord's Prayer, it would seem that we agree with God to forfeit His forgiveness if we do not forgive those who have hurt us (see Matthew 6:12). At the end of the Lord's Prayer,

Jesus made sure we get the message by reiterating His teaching on forgiveness and forcing us to take note of the penalty for unforgiveness (see Matthew 6:14–15).

A glance in a concordance at the occurrences of the words *forgive* and *forgiveness* shows the importance God puts on forgiving—both His forgiveness of us and our need to forgive others. According to the parable of the unforgiving servant (see Matthew 18:23–35), the unforgiving person will be punished severely. We are, then, to follow Jesus' example from the cross, where He prayed, "Forgive them, Father! They don't know what they are doing" (Luke 23:34).

Unforgiveness is not the only response that gives the enemy a legal right to enter and live within a person. Many people inherit demons that were given a legal right in a previous generation. I have ministered to dozens of individuals whose parents or grandparents were members of occult organizations such as Freemasonry or Mormonism or of non-Christian religions. With very few exceptions, these people have been carrying demons inherited from their forebears.

Many invite demons in, giving them legal rights through disobedience to God's laws. Implied in Ephesians 4:26–27 is the fact that if we wallow in anger we give the enemy a legal right to influence us. Hanging on to our anger is disobeying God and therefore is sin. So is wallowing in such things as fear, shame, rejection, lust, self-condemnation, rebellion, death wishes, hatred and a myriad of other negative emotions. The same is true of homosexuality, abortion, contemplating suicide, anger at God, witchcraft and belonging to occult organizations.

Whether by wallowing in negative emotions or through inheriting or inviting demons, people give legal rights to evil spirits. This means they have a right to inhabit a person and will stay until their legal rights are taken away.

Can Christians Be Demonized?

To date I have counseled more than two thousand people who were carrying demons, nearly all of them people of deep Christian faith. Contrary to the belief of many who have not had experience dealing with demonized people, Christians can and frequently do carry demons, usually left over from their pre-Christian days.

For those who are skeptical about Christians carrying demons, we can point out that those who came to Jesus for deliverance came in faith that He could help them. I believe that most if not all of them would classify as people of faith and fit into the category "Christian."

The early Church believed that everyone who came to Christ out of the world was carrying demons. Therefore, they required new converts to go through a preparation time, sometimes up to two or more years, during which they received instruction and underwent deliverance from demons. Only after the church leaders were sure the potential member was free of demons would they baptize him or her.[1] My experience would seem to confirm their assumption that demons live in nearly everyone.

This fact presents to us the necessity of developing a theory as to how this can be. My theory is that when a person comes to Christ his or her spirit, the central part of a person, becomes cleansed of sin and of any demons. The other four parts of a person (body, mind, emotions and will), though, may still carry demons. When a demonized person comes to Christ, the demons have to vacate the person's spirit; the Holy Spirit comes to dwell there. Demons, however, can still live in the other four parts. An important part of the Christian's growth, then, is taking these other parts for Jesus.[2]

Most of the people who come to me for ministry, though they are Christians, are carrying demons. Usually they have inherited some of the demons and have let others in through various kinds of disobedience during their pre-Christian years. Fortunately, if a person carrying demons is growing in his or her relationship with Jesus, the demons get progressively weaker. But in spite of this weakening, they usually do not leave on their own. They need to be cast out.

The need for deliverance from demons does not call into question a believer's salvation. A person who accepts Jesus as Savior and Lord is saved, whether or not he or she is carrying demons. If demons are present, they may hinder the Christian in various ways, but they cannot take away the person's salvation. Though demons can live in all five parts of a non-Christian, they cannot live in that central part of a Christian that we call the spirit. This is the part of us that lives forever and in which the Holy Spirit comes to dwell.

I have asked dozens of demons if they are living in a Christian client's spirit. First I ask, "Did you used to live in this person's spirit?" They answer, "Yes." Then I ask, "Do you live there now?" They always reply, "No" or "Not now." So I ask, "When did you have to get out?" They respond, "When Jesus came in," or "When the Holy Spirit came in" or they give me the date of the person's conversion. Though we have to be careful how much credence we give to what demons tell us, they are quite consistent on this point when they are pressured by the Holy Spirit to give us truthful answers.

It appears that the part of us that died when Adam sinned, the part we call our "human spirit," can be the home of demons only until we give our lives to Jesus. When we come to the Lord He takes up residence in our spirit, making it a new nature; and we become alive with His life in the core of our being. At that time any enemy spirits have to leave our spirit. At salvation, a person's spirit is washed clean from sin. But after salvation we still have to deal with sin in the other four parts of us, and those carrying demons also have to deal with the demons in those same four parts.

None of us likes the fact that demons can inhabit Christians. But since God allows it, we have to deal with it. As John and Paula Sandford have noted,

> The fact is, [demonization] happens. We have exorcised hundreds of Spirit-filled Christians, some of whom have been not only Spirit-filled for many years but well recognized, powerful servants of the Lord! How this can be so I cannot fully explain, but that it has been is for us an incontestable fact of many years of grueling experience.[3]

For an in-depth study of demonization in Christians, see C. Fred Dickason's excellent book, *Demon Possession and the Christian*.[4]

The Term "Demonized"

I refer to people who are carrying demons as "demonized," never as "demon-possessed." By demonized, I mean simply that a person is inhabited by one or more demons. Unfortunately, many Bible translations have used the term "demon-possessed" (see Matthew 8:28; 12:22). This is an unwarranted translation of one of the two Greek expressions used in the New Testament, each of which means simply "have a demon."

The translation "demon-possessed" is misleading and even dangerous since it gives the impression that the enemy has complete control over a person. While demons inside a person may be quite strong, they never have complete control of a person 100 percent of the time. Whether weak or strong, a demon will exert considerable control on some occasions and virtually none at other times. For this reason it is best to use a term that does not imply complete control.

The satanic kingdom is sterile; it has to work with things already in existence. Demons, therefore, seek to take advantage of a person's area of vulnerability. Upon finding such an area, they tempt a person to submit to weaknesses or misuse strengths. They like to keep people ignorant of their presence, since the most effective enemy is one you cannot identify. So the key to fighting an enemy lies in understanding how he operates.

Demons push people to such things as fear, anger, bitterness, rejection, self-hatred, unforgiveness, lust, shame, guilt, perversions and compulsions of various kinds—or whatever else to which a person is prone. When people obey them by submitting to the temptation, demons try to get them to blame themselves, as if they made the mistake all by themselves.

Counseling or Deliverance?

A major problem for those of us in the West is that our worldview assumes that every effect has a single cause. Therefore, if a person is having problems that we suspect are demonic, our assumption is that the demons are responsible for the problems. People frequently ask me, for example, "Is this problem emotional or demonic?" Their assumption is that if it is emotional, it is to be dealt with through counseling. If, on the other hand, it is demonic, it is to be dealt with through deliverance.

I have dealt with a steady stream of clients who have undergone years of therapy with professional counselors but have very little to show for it. Oftentimes they have learned what to call their problems and have gained an expensive friend (the counselor) who can advise and support them as they learn to live with their problems. But though they have learned to handle their problems better, they have not gotten completely free from those problems.

When this happens, I suggest the reason is because there is not enough power in the counselor's use of psychological techniques to bring about freedom. Although the techniques are clever and insightful, the only power to implement them is human power. Technique with only human power has severe limitations. And even Christian counselors, unfortunately, often use their insights in a very secular way, largely devoid of any but human power.

Likewise, I have dealt with many people who have assumed their problems are demonic and have gone to those who practice deliverance from demons for help. They often describe long, loud "knock down, drag out" public sessions, in which there was a lot of violence and, often, throwing up, resulting in much embarrassment and very little relief. Though the demons put on quite a show and my clients saw and experienced a lot of power, both from the demons and from God, these individuals testify that most of the problems they assumed were demonic are still with them.

Thus, over the years I have worked with a large number of clients who have experienced either counseling without deliverance or deliverance without counseling. And each person was about half-healed. Those who have undergone counseling without deliverance often show symptoms of demonization. In the case of those who have undergone deliverance without counseling, I often find emotional problems that remain even though the demons might be gone.

Could There Be Two Causes?

Though the idea of something having two causes challenges our worldview assumptions, that seems to be the reality here. The answer to the question of whether a person's problems are emotional or demonic seems to be "Yes—both." And the one is tied closely to the other, because most emotional and spiritual problems seem to give the enemy legal rights. As previously mentioned, anger is an emotional problem, though not a sin if dealt with right away (see Ephesians 4:26–27). But if anger is held on to, resulting in unforgiveness, it gives the enemy the legal right he needs to live inside a person. The same is true of fear, shame, guilt, rejection and a myriad of other emotional problems.

So when a person is having emotional problems, demons are very likely attached to those problems. And when a person suspects that he or she is experiencing demonic problems, there are likely emotional and/or spiritual problems giving the demons their rights. If demons are present, there is a reason; and that reason is found in the person's psychological and spiritual problems.

Thus, we have two causes for nearly all the emotional and spiritual problems we need to address. And each approach by itself deals with approximately half of what needs to be treated.

Rats and Garbage

The best analogy I know of is to see the demons as "rats" and the emotional and spiritual problems as "garbage." Demons are like rats: They go for garbage. The emotional and spiritual stuff is the garbage. As long as there is garbage, there are likely to be rats feeding on it.

If we have garbage in our homes, it attracts rats. If we are to get rid of the rats, we first need to deal with the garbage. If we fight the rats but keep the garbage, the rats come right back. But if we deal with the garbage, it is comparatively easy to get rid of the rats, though they do not usually go away without being chased. I have met many weak demons who were able to remain in their hosts, even after the garbage was gone, until someone kicked them out.

Demons can infest any of the emotional and spiritual stuff that I am referring to as garbage, and therefore most of those who have emotional or spiritual problems are carrying demons. The demonic rats inhabit their wounds. Jesus said the enemy could not get Him because he could find nothing in Him (John 14:30: "He has nothing in Me," NKJV; "He has no hold on me," NIV). No demonic rats could get to Him because there was nothing to which they could attach themselves, nothing in Him to get a hold on. This is the ideal situation for us—to have nothing in us to which the enemy can attach himself.

Some who do deep-level healing choose to deal with the rats before the garbage. Though sometimes this is called for because the demons are interfering with the inner healing, I seldom find it advisable, since it usually results in fighting with the rats when they are strong and takes more time than if the garbage is dealt with first. Conversely, if the emotional and spiritual stuff is dealt with first, the demons become weak and usually can be cast out with little or no fighting.

So I choose to deal with the garbage first, recognizing that demons are a secondary problem. When the primary problem, the garbage, is dealt with first, the demons are so weakened that they are unable to cause violence or embarrass the client.

How the Rats Get In

As mentioned earlier, spirit beings, including demons, have to obey the laws God has built into the universe. These laws, like the law of gravity, operate in and affect our lives whether or not we know it. As Westerners, we are seriously disadvantaged by being ignorant of these laws, for they greatly affect our understanding of demons. As I said in *Defeating Dark Angels*:

Laws and principles in the spiritual realm are every bit as binding as those that operate in the physical realm. Even an unconscious invitation for demons to enter has the same effect as an unconscious breaking of the law of gravity. If we stumble, no matter how unconsciously, we fall because we are subject to the law of gravity. Or if we consciously declare that we don't believe in the law of gravity and defy it, we soon find we are subject to it whether we want to be or not. The same is true of spiritual laws. *Invite a demon, consciously or unconsciously, and you get a demon, whether or not you know what you are doing or even believe in demons.*[5]

There are at least five ways demons can enter a person's life.

1. *People can invite demons into their lives.* Individuals, usually in their pre-Christian days, might have consciously or unconsciously invited demons to enter them. One way that people have invited demons in, usually without realizing they were doing so, is by joining occult organizations such as Freemasonry, Scientology, Mormonism or even college sororities and fraternities that require secret commitments, or by getting into New Age. Thus, they have invited the demons attached to the organization or movement to live within them. As John and Mark Sandford warn,

It can take only a moment to become demonized—for example, just one séance. The first commandment is, "You shall have no other gods before me" (Exodus 20:3). Deuteronomy 18:10–11 forbids consulting occult sources. One who does so calls on a power other than God. Rest assured that if anyone from the dark side is nearby, it will answer that call for more than we bargained for! Or we need commit only one act of sexual perversion. If there happens to be a demon specializing in sexual sin anywhere in the vicinity (most likely in the sexual partner), it will probably enter.[6]

In addition to joining occult organizations, people may invite demons into their lives by such activities as 1) getting involved with certain rock groups and their music; 2) playing with Ouija boards; 3) attendance at séances; 4) playing games such as Dungeons & Dragons, "Light as a feather, stiff as a board" (also known as party levitation), or table tilting; 5) going to psychics; and 6) playing mirror games such as Bloody Mary.

2. *There seems to be a law of the universe that allows demons to be inherited.* Apparently the demons of one generation can also be passed down. This is something I have struggled with, as it does not seem fair that an innocent newborn would enter the world demonized. Yet I run into this repeatedly, as I have to cast demons out of the children and grandchildren of people who have become demonized through their participation in occult organizations. The vows and curses of Freemasons and other occult organizations apply both to themselves and their families, thus allowing demonic infestation to be passed from generation to generation. It is my experience that, without fail, the children of Freemasons and adherents of Scientology, Mormonism and other occult organizations carry demonic spirits even if they have not participated in the organizations themselves.

In addition to occult demons, almost every other type of demon can be passed on through inheritance. This often results in the passing on of the negative emotional or even physical characteristics of one's parents or grandparents. The same is true of spirits of fear, death, pornography, rejection, hate, rage, homosexuality, cancer, diabetes and just about any other spirit.

3. *Demons can be invited in by someone in authority over another person.* Those in authority over others, such as par-

ents and domineering group leaders, can use their authority to bring about demonization.

I remember a ministry session in which I was dealing with a demon that had an especially strong grip on a young woman. I asked the demon what right it had to be there; and it replied, "Her mother gave her to me." When this woman was a young child, her mother dabbled in witchcraft and dedicated her daughter to this demon. Since my client was an adult and had given her life to Christ, we simply asserted her authority and Jesus' authority to break her mother's authority. We then were easily able to cast out the demon.

In another instance I ministered to a man whose nanny had given him to a demon. This man had lived in a Latin American country when he was a child, and his parents had entrusted him to a native nanny while they were working. This woman, either because she deliberately wanted to infect his family or because she did not know any other way to help the boy when he became ill, gave him to the spirit. Since she had been given authority over the child by his parents, her authority was sufficient to allow him to get demonized. Again, we were able to take that authority away from the demon and to free the man. The satanic world takes such authority very seriously and is able to infect many through it.

Many non-Western peoples routinely dedicate their children to clan or tribal gods or spirits before or at birth. It is customary, for example, for Chinese parents and grandparents to take a written record of the date and time of birth of a newborn to a temple to be blessed by (and dedicated to) a god. While their intent is to gain protection and blessing for the child, actually they are putting him or her under the authority of evil spirits. Many Christians in these societies have inherited the demons resulting from the dedications of past generations.

4. *Demonization can result from wallowing in negative reactions to emotional wounds.* As I have mentioned, retaining negative reactions to abuse—such as anger, bitterness, unforgiveness and self-rejection—gives demons a legal right to live in a person. The vast majority of the demons I have dealt with have received their rights through permission given by clients who have wallowed in such negative reactions.

When Paul cautioned, "Do not stay angry all day [lest you] give the Devil a chance" (Ephesians 4:26–27), he was warning us against giving the enemy a foothold by harboring any of the negative responses we deal with in deep-level healing. A person who harbors such feelings invites, though usually unconsciously, the demons that legally attach themselves to that person.

The focus of deep-level healing, therefore, is to enable people to deal with their emotional and spiritual problems, in order to get them healed, and to get rid of any and all demons attached to those problems.

5. *Unconfessed sin can also lead to demonization.* When we hide sin, we are in grave danger of becoming demonized. Hidden, unconfessed sin gives the enemy the right to enter and live within us. Though we tend to define sin too narrowly, it is sin that underlies every one of the issues that gives the enemy rights.

The satanic kingdom specializes in accusing people and getting them to wallow in self-blame, even after a sin or negative reaction has been forgiven. Enemy spirits even get many individuals to feel guilty for things that are not their fault. The sins of hanging on to forgiven guilt or of accepting undeserved guilt, then, function as important sources of the garbage that allows demonization. This may be further complicated by the self-blame that many feel for being demonized. As we minister, therefore, we need to be very careful not to unwittingly add to the guilt of those to whom we minister and thus add to the grip the enemy has on them.

What Allows Demons to Stay?

1. *Our Western worldview is a major factor in allowing demons to do their work.* The ignorance, and even denial, in our society regarding the existence of demons allows them to go unnoticed. If a problem is to be solved, it must first be recognized and acknowledged. As Westerners, we view ourselves as "enlightened," and the thought of the presence of demons or any other spiritual beings is something we have relegated to tribal societies "that don't know any better." Westerners view such people as ignorant and ruled by superstition and make-believe. We laugh when we hear stories of gremlins, ghosts and goblins on the prowl at Halloween. We view fairy tales that involve spirits as flights of imagination suitable only for children.

Many Westerners, including Christians, discount the stories missionaries tell about strange beliefs and events in other lands. There must be rational, nonsupernatural explanations for these events, they assume. Even some theologians and preachers, who are considered biblically orthodox, ignore or explain away the activities of spiritual beings recorded in Scripture. Most of them would not know what to do if the demons within a demonized person began to manifest themselves in their classrooms or churches.

Western Christians have developed various theories to avoid taking the spirit world seriously. Some have assumed that Jesus got rid of demons once and for all. Others believe that, though demons may be active in other societies, our "Christian" society is at least mostly free of them. Many pastors, Bible school and seminary professors and even entire denominations perpetuate the myth that Christians cannot be demonized. People with experience in dealing with demons know this to be untrue, of course. And some who believe in demonization keep that belief to themselves, lest they be considered kooks.

Many of our churches and Christian training institutions seem to have accepted such secular Western assumptions as "If you can't see it, it either doesn't exist or cannot be very important" and "If a thing can be explained naturalistically, neither God nor Satan are involved." We claim to have a biblical worldview, but we side with the West in denying most of the spiritual realities portrayed in the Bible.

Though at least one-third of Jesus' public ministry consisted of delivering people from demons, most Western churches and training institutions spend no time even teaching on the subject, much less freeing people from demons. Should we not be spending our time and energy on the things Jesus felt were most important?

Unfortunately, many non-Westerners, having been taught Western worldview assumptions in schools, also have come to deny or ignore these spiritual realities. When we have anti-supernaturalistic understandings, the emissaries of Satan can work freely right under our noses with the assurance that, whatever they do, either we will not notice or we will explain it some other way. The most effective enemy is the one that goes undetected. So, in Western and even certain segments of non-Western societies, demons can do pretty much whatever they have a legal right to do without being discovered.

2. *Our ignorance concerning the ways in which the enemy does his job is a contributing factor in allowing demons to stay.* Satan likes to keep us ignorant. Even Christians who believe that demons exist and are active are usually ignorant of how they work. Consequently, many have demons living within them without being able to discover that they are there.

They interpret difficulties in their lives naturalistically, as if there is no spirit world and no spiritual warfare. And they get discouraged because they have no answers.

3. *A number of people never deal with their internal garbage.* Even Christians often feel this is just the way things are to be for them, their lot in life. They have never known freedom and do not know how to obtain it. And oftentimes the only answers the Church gives are secular. Knowing little of the power of God to heal, pastors and church leaders advise people who are struggling to go to secular counselors or to Christians who do secular counseling without working in prayer power as do inner healers. So neither the garbage nor the demons get dealt with effectively.

Thank God there is a growing number of counselors, formally trained and untrained, who are learning to use their gifts and training to work in Jesus' power. (A number of these are listed in Appendix B.) The need, however, is still far greater than the available manpower.

4. *Some people suspect they have demons but are unable to get help.* They may go to their pastors but find they do not know what to do. Unfortunately, our pastors and other church leaders usually have a discouraging inability to deal with issues of emotional garbage and demonization. And those who do know how to deal with them are overworked.

Plus, some who do deal with demons are so loud, demonstrative and strange that many who need help refuse to go to them. Or if they go to them, they may be so mistreated and embarrassed that the experience is quite negative; and furthermore, they may not get free.

5. *Some people who have demons choose to keep them.* Sometimes demons give people special abilities of knowledge or control, or they persuade their hosts that they have special

protection. If the person in whom the demons live considers getting rid of them, that individual will hear lies such as "If you get rid of me, there goes your ability to control people or to know things others don't know"; or "You will lose all of your protection if you abandon me"; or "Your anger is your strength."

I once was asked to minister to a girl, whom I will call Ginny, who had the ability to cause a fellow member of her high school swimming team to get sick. Ginny did not get to swim in meets unless the girl above her could not compete. But she discovered that she could wish the other girl to get sick. This resulted in Ginny getting to take her place in the meets. I told Ginny that her power was satanic and that we could get rid of it so that she would be free. She refused, however, saying, "I don't want to get rid of this power. I'm enjoying it."

For many, such advantages are hard to risk losing. So they feel, as did Ginny, that they would rather keep the demons. It is a sad thing when people give up the chance for freedom to test the truth of the demon's predictions. When such is the case, we need to lead our clients to understand that there is no demonic power, knowledge or protection that is better than freedom in Jesus.

Demons Are Always a Secondary Problem

An implication of what I am saying about the relationship between rats and garbage is that there is a primary problem and a secondary problem. If rats are being attracted to garbage, the garbage is the primary problem. The rats are secondary, there only because the garbage gives them legal rights. If the things that give them legal rights are taken away, the rats are easily dismissed.

This means that those who challenge demons first (that is, before the garbage is dealt with) and fight to get rid of them are going about things the wrong way. It is easy to assume, probably because the spiritual dimension is so poorly understood, that when demons are present they are the major problem. This is a mistake; the primary problem is that which gives the demons their rights, not the demons themselves. Dealing with those things, however, is not as spectacular as dealing with the demons at their full strength. So deliverance specialists who seek notoriety gravitate toward dealing with the demons without paying much attention to the garbage.

I have had several invitations to conduct deliverance sessions to be recorded for airing on television programs. In response to each invitation, I have warned the producers that they likely would not see anything spectacular because I deal with the garbage first, thus weakening the demons so that they cannot put on a show. Only one of the groups felt it worthwhile to bring their equipment to record a deliverance session; and though it was a genuine deliverance, the TV people did not find anything they considered worth including in their program.

Counselors Sometimes Recognize the Problem

Not infrequently, either clients tell me they have been advised by professional counselors to come to me for deliverance or I am contacted by a counselor asking for advice. This happens when professional counselors recognize that they do not know how to deal with demonization. They may suspect a demon is involved. Or they may have heard of people who have gotten freedom from problems that had not resolved through counseling through deep-healing ministry. Or they simply may be trying to avoid the attention they might get from their supervisors or the accrediting agency if they are found to be dealing with demons.

Unfortunately, this recognition by professionals that they are not able to deal with certain issues, whether spiritual or emotional, has led some of them to turn to New Age approaches. They realize that though they may be skilled in their analysis and competent in applying good techniques, these abilities are often not adequate in and of themselves. They need more power. I have had clients complain to me that they were encouraged by a counselor to find a spirit guide or to engage in some other New Age technique in order to solve their problem(s).

Demonic Attachment and Strength

The amount of influence demons have on their hosts varies. There are strong demons and there are weak demons. Family demons and occult demons tend to be stronger than emotion spirits. Family demons are inherited from generation to generation, deriving their position from the fact that each newborn is dedicated to them. Occult demons result from occult practices and dedications to occult organizations. The emotion spirits are the most common, deriving their position from people's reactions to life events. We use function names for them, such as anger, shame, fear, rejection and the like.

Demons derive their power from whatever it is that gives them the legal right to be there—being dedicated to spirits as a child, wallowing in negative emotions, inheritance from a parent who belongs to an occult organization or a non-Christian religion, vows, curses and the like. In challenging a demon, we need to find out what legal ground it has in the person's life and, through inner healing, take that ground away.

As mentioned previously, the biggest problem is unforgiveness. If there is a lot of unforgiveness, anger, bitterness and the like, or if the person has been deeply involved in such things as pornography and sexual abuse, the demons will be strong. If a person continues to practice these attitudes and behaviors, the demons gain strength. When demons have been invited in by a person, they are likely to have quite a strong grip until that person renounces the invitation and cancels all authority given to the demons. Contrary to the belief of some, though, even then the demons seldom leave on their own. They need to be cast out.

When demons are present yet their host grows spiritually and emotionally, the demons' power is reduced. I have talked to many frustrated demons who could not do what they wanted to do because their host was "too close to Jesus." One demon of lust told me, "I can't get him to look! Whenever I bring a pretty girl across his path, he turns his head."

I assess the strength of demonic attachment on a scale of zero to ten. Weak attachment levels are zero to three, medium attachment levels are four to seven and strong attachment levels are eight to ten. The way to reduce the strength of the demons is to deal with the garbage. As we deal with the garbage, the hand on the dial immediately goes down. Sometimes when I begin ministering to a person I ask the demon how strong it is. One told me, "About a seven." After we had done some inner healing, I asked the question again. The reply: "A two." When the demon's power got down to zero, I kicked it out. This approach sees deliverance from demons as a subcategory of deep-level healing.

Though in Christians who are growing any demons will be weak, even then they can harass, confuse, engender guilt and contribute to many other annoying problems. Stronger demons can disrupt life even for Christians who appear to have things pretty well together. I recently delivered a Christian man of a very strong demon of anger whose assignment seemed to be the disruption of this man's marriage.

People seem to have various tolerances for demonic pressures. Some are able to endure quite a lot of pressure without buckling; others experience major interference from what seem to be very weak demons.

Don't Freak Out

Many people "freak out" when demons are mentioned, especially when we recognize how common it is for people to carry them. This should not be. Should an elephant get freaked out by a mouse? We are the spiritual elephants. We carry infinitely more power than demons. When we fight with them, we do not fight on equal terms. The power of the God of the universe is on our side. The demons are just angels.

It is wrong, however, to ignore them. For they are often there, doing their job to mess up human lives. And if people are to be free, they need to be freed from these alien beings as well as from their emotional and spiritual garbage.

For those who may need help in dealing with demons, I have listed in Appendix B several people and organizations that can be contacted. ISDM (International Society of Deliverance Ministers) is the largest of these organizations. It has several hundred informed deliverance ministers, most of whom recognize the need to do inner healing in order to get people completely free. The others on the list in Appendix B are likewise balanced in their approach.

So as we turn now to "Two Hours to Freedom," our plan is to deal with the demons. But not right away—first we want to take away that which gives them rights.

6

Two Hours to Freedom

In this chapter I will present the way I typically go about a deep-level healing ministry session, with the hope that it will provide a model for others. I am convinced that Jesus wants His followers to set captives free. But doing this does not seem to come naturally for most people, which suggests to me the need for a model to follow to get started in deep-level healing ministry.

I usually spend two hours in a ministry session. Though not everyone can get healed in two hours, I am amazed that most of my clients do not need more time than that. So I make two-hour appointments and systematically proceed through their lives according to the pattern described below, finding that people seldom need a second appointment.

The two hours are divided roughly into three segments. The first twenty minutes to half hour is spent getting acquainted, looking over the questionnaire I have had the person fill out (which you can see in Appendix A) and discussing any special problems. During the following hour I usually ask the Holy

Spirit to take the person back to conception and then to work from there through the memories up to the present. The last half hour, then, is spent kicking out the demons. I will detail each of these segments in the pages that follow.

Getting Acquainted

During the getting acquainted time, my aims are 1) to establish rapport, and 2) to get a feel for what the person's expectations—plus or minus apprehensions—are in coming to me. Establishing rapport is a matter of finding out who the person is and helping him or her to feel comfortable in what is probably a strange situation. I want my clients to trust me and to feel comfortable in opening up to me. When appropriate, I share things about myself and/or the ministry.

I often ask questions such as "What led you to come here?" or "What have you heard about what I do?" or "What is your relationship with Jesus?" Or I will pick up something on the questionnaire to ask about or ask, "What was your childhood like?" I don't want to get into situations in detail at this point, but I will often pick up clues as to where to focus special attention later when we get to particular places in the client's life history.

Sometimes during the getting acquainted time I find something that may block things later if not dealt with right away. In a recent ministry session a woman let me know during this time that she had had three abortions, two of which were to terminate pregnancies resulting from rape. It was obvious that she was so weighed down by guilt over the abortions that it would be difficult to focus on anything else. So I opted to deal with this situation before we started the inner healing.

I asked Jesus to give the woman a picture of each child in turn, so that she could guess what the sex was, name the baby, hold the baby, love him (she saw each as a boy) and apologize for aborting him. She rejoiced that Jesus was taking good care of her babies and that she would meet them and live with them for eternity. She then was able to complete the process she had been working on for years—forgiving herself—and lovingly she gave each baby to Jesus. Then we could begin the inner healing. The demon of death that had attached itself to the abortions was weakened during this exercise so that I could wait till I was dealing with the other demons to deal with it.

Back to the Womb

Once we have gotten acquainted a bit, I pray a prayer of gratefulness for the things God has done in the life of the client and request that He lead the client into new freedom during our session. I invite the Holy Spirit to take complete control and I forbid the enemy to interfere in what Jesus wants to do in this person's life. I then ask the client to close his or her eyes as I lead him or her, under the guidance of the Holy Spirit, back to prebirth memories.

Choosing What Jesus Chose

Since so many people are unhappy that they are who they are, I regularly focus first on making sure they choose what Jesus chose. I believe one of the implications of Ephesians 1:4 is that God (whom I picture as Jesus) chose just the right sperm and just the right egg to come together in our mother's womb. He chose one sperm out of hundreds of millions of sperm and one egg out of hundreds of eggs to bring about the miracle of conception. Though our parents chose the time and place where the conception would take place, it was Jesus' choice to give us life through this human act of sexual intercourse and His choice to use a specific sperm and a specific egg to make each one of us.

This being true, I ask clients to picture Jesus standing in front of them with His hands stretched out toward them, showing them a sperm in one hand and an egg in the other. I then ask if they agree that their conception was a good idea. Clients are often really upset deep down, either because they were conceived at all or because they turned out to be the gender that Jesus assigned them. There may be deep anger at God that hinders any quest for freedom and healing. So I work with clients to help them choose what Jesus chose, inviting them to choose even against their feelings in order to be on Jesus' side, working with Him toward freedom. Frequently, then, a significant change of attitude takes place when they picture themselves putting Jesus' hands together, resulting in their own conception. They have agreed with Jesus on a very basic feeling.

The distress over who they are is usually a reflection of their parents' attitude, and this choice is an attempt to break the unconscious spiritual power of the parental attitude. Parents commonly do not want to be pregnant at this time, or they want to be pregnant but desire a child of the other sex. If this is the case, the infant in the womb knows it and goes through gestation and birth knowing that he or she was not wanted.

The crucial thing here, then, is for clients to choose against their feelings of unwantedness and against their parents' feelings—choosing instead to agree with Jesus that what He wanted is what they want. As they picture themselves putting His hands together, they make this choice, agreeing that they were not a mistake to Jesus and blessing their own conception.

If there is no dissatisfaction on the client's part, the agreement with Jesus is something to celebrate. We thank Jesus for what He chose and rejoice that He brought about the client's conception and protected him or her through gestation. It is easy to bless our conception if we know and feel that we were wanted.

If there is dissatisfaction, I cancel any curse of unwantedness. A parental desire not to be pregnant, or for the child to be the opposite sex, or to terminate the pregnancy through abortion often constitutes a curse. So I say something like, "In the name of Jesus, I cancel any curse of unwantedness."

This part of our exercise can be very important, especially for those with low self-esteem, because the low self-esteem may be rooted in this unwantedness. I have had clients who were so down on themselves that they found it nearly impossible to picture themselves putting Jesus' hands together. There is a spiritual and emotional breakthrough, however, when they are able to make a conscious choice to accept themselves by choosing what Jesus chose. This breaks the enemy's power wielded through the person's negative attitude toward him- or herself.

Blessing the First Month

I then bless the very first month of my clients' existence *in utero* with peace—peace that (in memory) they are in the place where Jesus wants them to be, peace that their parents did God's will in bringing about their conception, peace in knowing that they are going to make it safely through gestation, childhood and into adulthood, and that Jesus is going to be with them all the way. I usually also bless them with joy and excitement over the journey they are embarking on in life and the sure knowledge that they are going to make it through whatever difficulties they face in life. We can say this because we know their future.

At this point, or at some later point, I will usually speak to the child about the fact that he or she was not alone in the womb. According to Psalm 139:13–16, God was there. The psalmist declares,

> You created every part of me; you put me together in my mother's womb. . . . When my bones were being formed, carefully put together in my mother's womb, when I was growing there in secret, you knew that I was there—you saw me before I was born.

And to Jeremiah, God said, "I chose you before I gave you life, and before you were born I selected you to be a prophet to the nations" (Jeremiah 1:5). God's hands were there: creating every part, putting each one of us together in our mother's womb, knowing us and seeing us before we were born, caring for us so gently, making sure every part was formed and loving us into existence.

Taking Authority over Ancestry

As we focus on the first month in the womb, I claim authority over my clients' ancestry through both of their parents. I deal with any enemy spirits that may have gotten into the family lines due to dedications, curses, sinful behavior or any other way.

I say something like, "In Jesus' name I cancel any rights the enemy has gained in John's father's family line through dedications, curses, sinful behavior or in any other way that have come down to John. I break this power at the point of his conception." I then do the same for the mother's family line.

It is quite common, as previously mentioned, for spirits to be inherited, especially by Asians, Africans, Native Americans and others brought up in non-Christian religions. We have authority to cancel their power, both at this point and later when dealing specifically with family demons. The person may or may not feel a release at this time. Knowing that I will come back to this later if it seems warranted, I do not pay much attention to whether or not this happens. I'm not sure why this part of the exercise seems to free some people from inherited demons but does not seem to free others.

Blessing Each Month

At this point I bless the preborn infant during each month of gestation, saying something like, "I bless you in the second month with peace." I bless the person with peace or some other specific gift as we go along, or I may simply speak a general blessing (e.g., "I bless you in the fifth month").

After blessing the person in the third month, I usually pause to ask how this feels. Most people respond that they feel peaceful. Some, however, experience negative emotions such as anger, fear or shame. If this is the case, I try to find out what might have led to that feeling and to get it healed. Often children in the womb need to give such feelings to Jesus or to forgive their parents. Sometimes I talk to the (memory of) the preborn children, explaining that their parents had a difficult childhood and had never gotten healed from their dysfunction. So the root of the problems the client is facing is mistakes or choices the parents made, not something the client has done. "But in spite of your problems," I will say, "you're going to make it. We know your future. And you can forgive your parents and give them and your damaged feelings to Jesus."

Based on the written questionnaire and the interview at the beginning of the session, I will have a pretty good idea of what the client's parents' relationship must have been like while the client was in the womb. If I suspect there was a lot of conflict between them, I speak to the preborn memory as if it were a person capable of hearing me. I speak comfort to the infant and point out that whatever is going on outside is the concern of the adults, not of the preborn child. The child is safe in the hands of Jesus, and all will be well through gestation and birth. In short, "Little one, you're okay and you're going to make it. Just rest with Jesus while the grown-ups do their thing."

This usually calms down the person and returns the peacefulness with which the preborn child started. If the person does not become calm and we cannot seem to find the reason, typically I go on to the next months and through birth, hoping that at some later stage of the ministry we will stumble upon whatever the problem was.

I go through the months in this way, usually stopping again at the sixth month to make sure the "memory baby" is still peaceful. When we get to the ninth month, I will usually speak the specific blessings again (e.g., peace, joy, excitement) and then invite the person to be born.

Occasionally demons will try to disrupt what we are doing. They know that they will get weaker as we take care of the garbage. If a demon disrupts, I command it to step aside and stop interfering with what Jesus is doing. This usually works, but if not I will go after the demon to reduce or break its power. I cancel all curses and take away all rights the demon has through inheritance. I have the person renounce everything we can think of that might give the demon power. Usually this weakens the demon enough that we can go back to the exercise and complete it without further interruption.

Birth

Next I ask clients to picture Jesus holding them at birth. I ask them how that feels—to which most respond quite positively—and if they can see Jesus' face. Some see Jesus with a loving, accepting expression on His face, while others just see His hands or arms holding the baby. Some are not able to picture Jesus at all, but still usually feel the peacefulness and security of being in His arms.

The aim of this part of the exercise is to help people feel the security of having Jesus with them at all times. When I ask them what it feels like to be in Jesus' arms, they usually mention things like security, strength with gentleness and happiness at both knowing and *feeling* Jesus' care for them.

I then ask my clients to picture themselves taking the infant from Jesus and holding the baby in their own arms. This is a special experience for most, though difficult for those with low self-image. One man saw himself take the baby and throw him on the floor! I usually ask the person to talk to the baby, expressing love, care and commitment to treat the child well as he or she faces the challenges of life ahead. It is important to work through any negative feelings at this point, since these experiences are foundational to what follows.

The purpose of this part of the exercise is to enable clients to bond with their younger selves if there have been issues or events that have hindered that bonding. It is surprising how many people are living with a kind of rift between their older self and their younger selves. This is where learning to love ourselves can start for those who do not already love themselves.

Sometimes demons try to interfere with this part of the ministry by causing pain, shaking or some other annoyance. They know that they will be weakened if these early issues are resolved. When this happens I usually command them to step aside until we get to them later. Usually they obey, but sometimes they refuse and have to be challenged at this early stage of the ministry. If this is the case, I ask them what they are connected to in the person's life. If they tell me what it is, we deal with it. (Usually it is the client's need to forgive someone.) If that does not work, I go over the breaking of inherited power and present curses, including self-curses, and do whatever else is necessary to get the demons out of the way.

Inner Persons

I usually follow up the "Back to the Womb" exercise by moving through the memories of childhood into adulthood. The best way I have found to do this is by treating the memories as inner persons and helping these inner parts to experience Jesus in the memories. The best "weapons" to get people healed are 1) for them to experience the presence of Jesus in each situation, and 2) the ability to promise the inner persons at each stage that we know their future, and therefore that they are going to "make it."

I approach the inner persons stage by stage, looking for hurtful experiences that they can share with Jesus. I want my clients, usually with their eyes still closed, to experience Jesus in the memories and to give Him their hurts. I want all the inner persons to forgive everyone who has hurt them. And usually they also have to forgive themselves and God. As with all emotional and spiritual healing, unforgiveness is the biggest crippler and needs to be dealt with thoroughly.

As the first step toward forgiving, I affirm the validity of my clients' negative feelings toward those who hurt them. I will often say something like this: "You have a right to be angry, even to hate and to seek revenge for what these people have done to you. But no matter what you do, you can't really get back at them. And if you try, there's a law in the universe that says you will be enslaved to those feelings. Only Jesus, as God, can get back at those who hurt you. So God says, in Romans 12:19, "Vengeance is mine, I will repay" (NKJV). Give them to Him, and He'll make you free.

Then I invite clients to forgive everyone they need to forgive at the ages at which hurts occurred. As noted earlier, I have found that forgiveness granted by the inner person at the younger age results in a deeper kind of forgiveness than when the client forgives as an adult.

In addition to unforgiveness, many other issues need to be given to Jesus. Many struggle with anger, depression, shame, guilt, fear, worry, rejection, self-hatred, lust and other sexual issues, occult involvement, curses and a myriad of other feelings developed in reaction to life experiences. These issues need to be dealt with at each of the following age levels.

Preschool Inner Children

Starting with the baby in the adult's arms, I invite clients to picture themselves as babies with Jesus holding one hand and their adult self holding the other—teaching the child to walk, then to talk. Most people cannot consciously recall these memories, but they can usually picture them. And we know they happened.

I then ask the person to picture the earliest memory she can recall, picturing Jesus with her in the event. The event may be positive, in which case I ask the inner person to rejoice, even dance, with Jesus. Or it may be negative, in which case I ask the person to give Jesus whatever unpleasant feelings come with the memory and to let Jesus hug her.

This is the time to give to Jesus any unforgiveness. It is also good for the adult to see himself hugging the child. Typically, doing this frequently helps a person learn to love himself.

The age of people's earliest memories varies greatly. Many can recall little or nothing before they started school. Some have blocked out this period because it was so painful; others just do not seem to be impressed enough by the events to be able to bring them into their consciousness. At any rate, I work with what the person *can* recall, knowing that things often come back later, especially if something is there that needs to be healed.

Elementary School Inner Children

The first day of school can be traumatic, especially if children do not have an older brother or sister to accompany them. So, we go to kindergarten and on up through the elementary grades, with Jesus—dealing with one experience after another involving teachers, classmates, friends and family in relation to each inner child. I like to look for at least one inner child in each grade (though seldom are there that many), always helping clients to experience Jesus in the memory and to give Him all their "stuff."

Each of the inner kids needs lots of hugs from Jesus and from the adult person as they grow up. Sometimes I suggest that several of the children are carrying backpacks full of negative emotions that they need to drop at Jesus' feet. I also encourage clients to picture their positive experiences and to receive hugs in those situations as well.

In each memory experience, I like to talk to the inner children as if they are real children. Normally they are very alive in the person and are able to interact and share whatever they are feeling. And the adult self will usually see them change their posture and attitude when hurts are healed. They become happy and often see themselves dancing or having a party with Jesus.

Key things to look for are the ways children were treated by parents and teachers (e.g., discipline, criticism versus encouragement), embarrassing experiences (e.g., wetting their pants, bringing home bad report cards), moving away from friends, changing schools, being bullied, getting into fights, being abandoned or betrayed by friends, seeing their parents fight, getting lost and a myriad of other typical experiences.

Inner Adolescents

We are sexual beings, so we dare not neglect this part of our experiences. As we move along to middle school or junior high, then, there is often a lot to deal with in regard to the onset of puberty, especially for girls. There is usually a breakdown of understanding between youngster and parents during this time, even in the best of home situations. And the people I minister to often did not have good home situations. I continue to check each year, though there will not be an inner child every year and some especially eventful years may yield more than one inner child.

Inner persons at this age need careful handling, with lots of love and understanding and hugs—as we picture them dealing with changing bodies, the onset of menstruation and surging sexual urges, often met by strong adult (and church) opposition to release through masturbation. Adolescents frequently face awkwardness and dissatisfaction with their bodies; cliquishness and conflict with peers; sexual experimentation, often accompanied by emotional and sexual abuse; experimentation with drugs; and delving into occult teachings and practice. Many curse their bodies in general or specific parts of their bodies in particular, either in words or through involvement in anorexia and bulimia. And some get into cutting and/or contemplate or even attempt suicide.

It is critical that the inner adolescent experiences acceptance from the adult. Many adults are so ashamed of how they behaved as juveniles that they want to avoid going back to teenage memories. When problems are dealt with through inner person imagery, however, many people find it easier to face difficult memories. Wonderful things often happen when the adult pictures himself hugging his teenage self and forgiving him, or when the teenage inner person is helped to forgive those who hurt her.

Typically it is easier to talk to and get a response from a teenage inner person than a child inner person. And since I have found that the adolescents are often hiding something, I invite them to speak up and share their secrets so that we can deal with them.

For many it is more important to talk to and get a response from a teenage inner person than a child inner person. The issues are often weightier and the tendency to hide important things is often greater, leading to more resistance to deal with the issues. If clients have experienced success in dealing with childhood matters, however, they are usually more open to "letting it all hang out" as inner teenagers.

Inner Adults

Many of the teenage issues are relevant for adults as well. However, now we add problems related to marriage (or lack of it) and career. Sexual issues may still be prominent, as well as attitudes toward one's body. But the approach is the same: locate the inner persons at each age and in each hurtful experience and help them to experience Jesus and to give Him their hurts. We usually do not have to go year by year at this level, since the issues tend to cluster into types, enabling us to deal with the types of problems rather than each specific instance.

Wrap-up of Inner Person Experiences

As we go through the various stages, dealing with each of the problem areas, we find that each inner person becomes happy. As they give Jesus their loads, they get relieved; and the adult sees them sitting on Jesus' lap, or dancing and playing around Him, or near Jesus in some other happy situation.

As we wrap up this part of the ministry, I like to invite all the inner persons out—those surrounding Jesus as well as any who are not yet free to dance, stand or sit by Him. When the adult sees this, I often ask if any of the inner persons are still struggling, and, if so, if they would raise their hand so the adult can see them. If the client sees any raised hands, we go to the inner person(s) who is still struggling, find out what the problem(s) is and deal with it. When no more inner persons have their hands raised, but rather all of them are celebrating with Jesus, I know this part of the ministry is completed.

Kicking Out the Rats

During the last half hour of the ministry session, I turn to dealing with the demons. Remember, demons are like rats—rats who feed on garbage. *Demons are a secondary problem.* When we deal with the primary problem, the garbage, the demons lose their power, though they seldom if ever leave until they are cast out. The garbage has been taken care of; the backpacks full of garbage have been laid at the feet of Jesus. Now it is time to kick out the rats.

As I have been leading the person through the various events at the various stages of life, I have been listing demonic "suspects" on my notepad. Their presence is usually quite predictable once one knows a few rules. So when the inner healing has come to this point, I ask the person's permission to challenge the demons that I pretty well know are there, since their names are on my list.

The basic rule is that whenever a person has held on to a damaged emotion, a demon has a legal right to attach itself to that emotion. Most of the people who come to me for deep-level healing have wallowed in one or more damaged emotions, and therefore are carrying demons. In many instances, however, they have grown in their Christian faith and thus weakened the demons. Their own growth, then, plus the inner healing usually have weakened the demons so much that they rarely are able to cause any disturbance or violence.

Commanding Them to Go

The demon that appears most frequently on my list is Anger, typically along with its helpers Bitterness, Resentment, Depression and sometimes Rage. They are there because the person has held on to the emotion of anger and the feelings these other labels suggest. I label the demons that attach themselves to these emotions by the same names as the emotions. That is, the emotion of anger, if held on to, attracts a demon of anger—which I call "Anger."

In Ephesians 4:26–27 we are told that if we keep anger past the day's end we are in danger of giving Satan a foothold. The implication of these verses is that we *will* get angry (even Jesus got angry), but if we do not hold on to it, it is not a sin and the devil is not given a chance to inhabit us. If we do hold on to it, though, a demon gains a legal right to come live within us. Likewise with most every other negative emotion—keep it and a demon has a right to come.

Knowing this, as I listen to my clients' garbage I usually quite easily come up with a list of suspects based on the emotions the clients have held on to in reaction to the events in their lives. The other demons that I find most often are

Shame (along with Guilt, Deception and Lying Spirits), Fear (along with Worry, Anxiety and Panic), Rejection (along with Abandonment and Neglect), Hate (along with Self-Hatred), Lust (along with Pornography, Fantasy and Adultery), Death (along with Suicide, Death Wish, Infirmity and other spirits that attack the body, Drug Spirits, Anorexia, Bulimia, Alcoholism, Nicotine and other spirits that push people toward death), Occult Spirits (e.g., New Age, Ouija Board, Fortune Telling), and Cult or Religion Spirits (e.g., Freemasonry, Mormonism, Islam, Scientology, Buddhism).

With the client's permission, then, I command all enemy spirits, with all of their helpers, to line up in the presence of Jesus. After that I ask the angels (or Jesus) to prepare a series of locked boxes in which to collect the demons. I want to collect them group by group in the locked boxes and then send them all to Jesus at once.

Since many clients have self-image problems related to shame (feeling bad about who they are), I often challenge Shame first. Its helper Guilt attaches to those who feel bad over something they have done. And their helper Deception specializes in lying and misleading its victims to hold on to shame and guilt. If these issues have been taken care of during the inner healing, I often can easily command Deception to speak the lies it has been telling the client. I usually pump this spirit for some of these lies so the person will know where they have come from. I then bind these three demons (Shame, Guilt and Deception, along with the Lying Spirits) and command them to get into a locked box. If one or more of them will not get in the box, we may have to go back to some of the life experiences in which the client needs to give these feelings to Jesus. When this is taken care of, the power of the demons is taken away and they get into the box, ready to be sent to Jesus.

When one group of spirits is safely in its box, I turn to another group—for example, Fear and its helpers Worry, Anxiety and Panic—and do the same thing, getting that group into another box. Next I might tackle Anger and its helpers Bitterness, Resentment, Depression and Rage. If these demons will not go easily, it is often because the person still needs to forgive someone. Frequently the spirit of Anger, if commanded, will tell the client whom he or she needs to forgive. When forgiveness is given, then, Anger and its comrades usually go easily.

And so on with each group on my list. When I have come to the end of the list, I ask the angels to round up any spirits we have not yet found and to force them into another box— on the count of three. I don't know why, but demons seem to move faster when I count to three!

Sending Them to Jesus

When all the demons are in boxes, I ask the angels to take the boxes to Jesus and ask Him to dispose of them, sending them away from the client as far as the east is from the west. I also ask Jesus to show clients what He does with the boxes, so that they know the boxes have been discarded. People often see them thrown or kicked into nothingness, or into the sea, or into fire or into a bottomless pit.

When the boxes full of spirits have disappeared, I ask Jesus to plant His cross and His empty tomb between the client and the spirits, forbidding the demons ever to come back or to send any others.

Next I ask Jesus to fill all of the empty spaces resulting from the demons' departure with His peace. I often then bless the person with love (for Jesus, self, others), patience, strength, joy or other blessings that come to mind. Sometimes I ask Jesus to seal what He has done, thus preventing anything that has been accomplished from being reversed.

With this the session is over, except for dealing with the habits discussed in the next chapter. These two hours are all the time most people need to spend with me. They can work on changing habits on their own, sometimes with help from a professional counselor. Some individuals, however, need one or more additional sessions to deal with things we may have missed during the two hours—things they may not have mentioned or demons we may have overlooked. If they have a background in the occult, they may need several sessions.

But for most people the two-hour session is enough to launch them into a new era of freedom. I am amazed at what the Holy Spirit does in such a short time. I have not done the research to prove the effectiveness of this ministry, but my impression is that at least 90 percent of my clients have some change in a positive direction and at least 75 percent are radically changed. Though based on reports from clients and my personal observation, I believe these figures are probably close to what research would show.

A Postscript: Practical Q and A

People often ask practical questions such as the following:

Q. Can everyone do this ministry in two hours?

A. Probably not, at least at first. It may take a while to gain the expertise to get it down to two hours. In the early days of your ministry you likely will not be able to control the time as well as you will be able to eventually. It is easy to let the client go on and on telling his or her story or talking about various things. You must keep the person on track, *dealing* with feelings rather than just thinking and talking about them. This is an *experiential* ministry (see next question).

Q. What is the basic difference between this ministry and professional counseling?

A. *This ministry is experiential, not merely cognitive.* People don't get healed by *talking about* their problems. They get healed only by *experiencing* Jesus' presence (through picturing, to be sure) in the events in which the damage occurred; and it is often difficult for people to shift from what they are familiar with—thinking and talking—to *experiencing* through picturing and feeling. Professional counseling is sometimes called "talking therapy" because it specializes in talking about problems. The talking may be enlightening, but it does not heal. Experiencing Jesus heals.

Q. What if people can't picture?

A. This is a problem for surprisingly few people (including myself). Women and right-brained men usually have the easiest time. Men and left-brained people of either gender often have trouble, at least at first. I try to get them to *feel* and then report their feelings as we go back to the memories. I have had some success with having people merely *think their way through the exercises*, putting the focus on reexperiencing the events with Jesus. They usually begin picturing somewhere along the way. When we deal with demons, it is usually very helpful to be able to picture the demons in the boxes as we send them to Jesus.

Q. What about gifting?

A. I believe in spiritual gifts, but I have proven through my own ministry, I think, that special gifting is not necessary. I do not have what I call "spectacular gifting." I seldom get words of knowledge and almost never get pictures or prophecies. I just go at things systematically, claiming the presence and power of the Holy Spirit promised to us by Jesus (see John 14:12)—and God does wonderful things. It is nice to have spectacular gifting, but it may get in your way if you don't watch out.

Q. Shouldn't we work in teams?

A. Yes indeed. I work alone most of the time, but I am not proud of the fact. People make appointments to see me in my office, so forming a team is seldom practical. My preference, however, is to work with a team of three—one to lead, one to intercede and one to take notes. Especially in the early stages of your ministry, by all means work in teams. This gives you multiple insights and giftings.

Q. Is it okay to minister alone to members of the opposite sex?

A. We should never work alone with a person of the opposite sex if we can help it. This isn't much of an issue for those who minister in teams. Since I work alone, I ask female clients to bring a friend. They usually do. But if they don't, I am very careful. And I am thankful that my age helps me to be less susceptible to temptation than would have been the case when I was younger.

Q. What if a demon gets physical?

A. We make the rules. One of my rules is not to engage a demon physically because that establishes that it will be a physical battle. Our power is in the Holy Spirit, wielded through words. There have been several times when a demon challenged me physically. But I refused to engage the demon physically, choosing instead only to speak, even when a client held a razor blade in her hand and was cutting herself with it. At my repeated command, she finally dropped the razor blade. On another occasion I could not get the demon to allow me to speak to the client; so I, along with my team, went out for lunch. When we came back the demon was no longer in charge, so we were able to speak to the person, deal with his stuff and gain the power we needed to cast out the demon.

Q. What if things get out of hand or require experience beyond my depth?

A. Shut the ministry down for now. Make it a rule not to go over three hours in any given session. If demons are the problem, command them into a box until approached again in the name of Jesus, and terminate the session. Then call someone with greater expertise than you, such as those on the list in Appendix B.

See my book *Defeating Dark Angels* for additional questions and answers, particularly in regard to demonic tactics.

7

Habits

When Lisa came to me, she had been recently diagnosed with cancer. The fourth daughter in her Chinese family, it didn't take a rocket scientist to figure out that Lisa, now in her late thirties, was not wanted by her parents. So I asked her if she had ever tried to be a boy. "Every second of my life," she spit out.

Lisa had wanted so much to be a boy that as her breasts developed, she strapped them tight against her body to keep people from discovering that she was a female. I asked Lisa if she had ever cursed her body. "Thousands of times," she answered. She had spoken hateful things to her breasts, hips, hair and other parts of her body.

We dealt with these and a number of other issues. After we cancelled the curses, Lisa began to accept and love herself as the person Jesus planned her to be. Then I said, "Now comes the hard part!" I explained to Lisa the importance of dealing with the habits she had built up over the years. I asked her if she had a full-length mirror. Learning that she did, I suggested that she stand naked in front of that mirror each day, blessing her body and especially those parts that she hated most.

Getting free is one thing; maintaining that freedom can be as much of a challenge. Although God takes away the emotional hurts as we go through the inner healing process, He seldom takes away the habits that have kept us bound. We usually have to work with Him to conquer those habits after the roots have been dealt with and we have gotten free from the hurts. Why God doesn't do the job all at once, I don't know. I just know that the challenge of overcoming the habits is usually a second problem for people.

One time a demon scoffed at me and said, "You humans— you do our job for us!" That appears to be the case for many people. The only thing demons seem to have to do oftentimes is plant a lie within us and train us to tell ourselves the lie. We have a habit that empowers the lie and keeps our negative attitude toward ourselves in place.

What was important for Lisa was to use her freedom to break the lifelong habit of self-hatred. We had gotten the roots of that habit healed. Choosing against her strongly held feeling that she was a mistake, Lisa had been able to agree with Jesus that it was good for her to be a female. She could, as an adult, understand the cultural pressures on her parents to produce a boy. And she could communicate to her inner selves both the problem of the cultural pressure and the truth that Jesus wanted her to be female. She could then invite her younger parts to join her adult self in choosing what Jesus wanted. This freed her to accept and even glory in her femaleness.

We had also canceled the curses Lisa had put on herself. I let her know that the one who pronounces the curses owns the curses, and can therefore cancel them. As Lisa renounced the curses she had put on herself—on her body, mind and emotions—the curses were broken and she was free to work on her habits.

Lisa took my advice about working on her attitude toward her body while standing before a full-length mirror. I received a letter from her about two years later saying that the cancer was gone. I do not know the details of what happened during those two years, but I am sure that Lisa's physical healing came as part of the process of her working to overcome her habits once she had gotten free emotionally and spiritually.

Habits Empower

Christians talk a lot about God's power and Satan's power, but they seldom mention the human power of a person who participates with God or Satan. The human power lies initially in the choices we make, and it is carried on in the habits that keep those choices in force. Both God's power and Satan's power, then, piggyback on human habit. Habits can be hard to break. But if we work with God at breaking them, they are easier to break once the roots have been disposed of through inner healing.

As with all of our interactions with Jesus (or with Satan), our will is a crucial element. Just as the way we use our will is key to our working with Jesus to get healed, so it is key to breaking old habits and establishing new ones. If people are to get completely free, they need to do whatever is necessary to work with God, both in the healing process and in the development of "freedom habits." God's principle is *partnership*. Whether it is for salvation, for healing or for breaking habits, God works *with* us. He usually does not do things in the human arena by Himself.[1]

But even after they have participated with God in getting free, many Christians expect God to do the follow-up work alone. Hopefully they have learned that neither salvation nor deep-level healing can happen without their choosing continually to work in partnership with God. Now they must learn that the same partnership needs to be employed to break the old habits and establish new ones.

God is willing and eager to heal and free us if we will work with Him. He loves to heal, but He wants us to do our part, to work *with* Him. He takes our emotional baggage only if we choose to give it to Him. He also takes our habits if we choose to give them to Him. This may take longer than did the healing, and may take more work.

I have had people come back weeks or months after great deep-level healing sessions to tell me how hard things are now. They know they have been genuinely freed, but they share how intense the battle has been—not against demons or the heavy emotional and spiritual problems they originally came to get free from, but against the present threat of falling back into old habits. They have needed to be on guard at all times lest they slip back into the old patterns.

As I have said, habits are notoriously hard to break. There is great human power in habits, often enhanced by demonic power and the emotional garbage in our lives. But once the roots empowering the habits are healed and any demons attached to them are forced to leave, breaking the habits is much easier. That is not to say that the habits are easy to break—just easier than while the roots were still firmly supporting them.

Post-Ministry Instruction

I want people to retain the freedom God brought to them during our deep-level healing sessions. Many clients will automatically do what they need to do next; many others, however, will need help regarding what to expect and what to do about it. They may find old habits to be tenacious as they try to conquer them. In addition, demons that have been cast out will often try to harass their former hosts and to convince them that nothing has changed. Though now outside of us, they would like us to believe they are still inside and still have power over us. New "freedom habits" need to be developed, and clients need to assert the authority they have in Christ to chase away any harassing demons.

Practicing Newness

As with any attempt to change, we need to practice. It is important to confront the old attitudes and habits by aggressively doing something to replace them. The "mirror treatment" (whether naked or clothed) that I encouraged Lisa to use is an effective way to confront self-hatred (or self-rejection, self-condemnation or self-loathing). I used it myself to confront the self-hatred I lived with for about fifty years. I simply looked at myself in the mirror from time to time and said, either out loud or to myself, "I love you!" This was extremely difficult for me—at first I had to wink as I said the words! But I forced myself to do it, and it worked. Changing our volition, or will, is hard work, but it's worth it.

After months of doing this I found that I began to feel favorably about myself. This in itself was a huge thing for me. But the more exciting thing that happened after a couple of years was a big surprise. I looked at myself one day, enjoying my new attitude toward myself, and all of a sudden the thought came, *I not only love you, I like you! Like* is above *love* in our attitude toward ourselves. We can choose to love ourselves, with little or no emotion. But it takes real, positive feeling to *like* ourselves. Surprisingly, I seemed to have crossed an invisible line from *love* to *like*. This feeling, then, had become an attitude—an attitude that has never left me.

The same kind of exercise can be used if the issue is self-forgiveness (guilt), shame, fear or most any other attitude we might have toward ourselves. The idea is to do something regularly that confronts the negative habit and replaces it with a positive one.

Talking to oneself in a mirror is the most effective way I have found to work on changing the habit of self-hatred or self-rejection. Suicidal tendencies, which are a form of self-hatred, can be dealt with by combining the mirror treatment with the relationship of an accountability partner.

Other habits may need other strategies. If a person's previous habit was using drugs or alcohol, he or she obviously needs to keep away from those substances. It is important to find something to take their place, and organizations are available to help with that.

Dealing with Demons

We can get rid of the demons living inside of us, but they still may be able to harass us. As mentioned earlier, though now outside of us, they may come back and try to convince us that they are still inside of us and still have power over us. With the authority we have in Christ, however, once we have been freed we can usually simply command the demons to be gone. I recommend people say something like "If this is the enemy, stop it!" or "In Jesus' name, be gone!"

One client of mine reported that the demons came back while he was asleep and started to assert themselves as if they had never left, saying, "We're back!" The man reported that he struggled a bit trying to get awake, but gathered enough presence of mind to ask, "Inside or outside?" The demons replied, "Outside"—whereupon the man simply said, "Then get out of here." The demons left, and he went back to sleep!

Clients need to know they have the same Holy Spirit, and therefore the same authority, as do those of us who practice this ministry regularly. All of us need to obey James's command, "Resist the devil and he will flee from you" (James 4:7, NKJV). Such resistance is usually enough, though it may not be effective immediately, and sometimes it takes a while to get free from the harassment. Sometimes the person will need additional prayer ministry.

All believers need to know their authority in Christ (see Luke 9:1; John 14:12) and to be able to assert their position in Him. The enemy has probably been lying to them for years about who they are. They can assert, on the authority of the Word of God, that they belong to Jesus.

> Those who are led by God's Spirit are God's children. For the Spirit that God has given you does not make you slaves and cause you to be afraid; instead, the Spirit makes you God's children. . . . God's Spirit joins himself to our spirits to declare that we are God's children. Since we are his children, we will possess the blessings he keeps for his people, and we will also possess with Christ what God has kept for him.
>
> Romans 8:14–17 (see also Galatians 4:4–7; 1 John 3:1–3)

We also are set apart to become like Jesus: "Those whom God had already chosen he also set apart to become like his Son" (Romans 8:29). In addition, we are called and chosen by Jesus to be His friends.

> I do not call you servants any longer, because servants do not know what their master is doing. Instead, I call you friends, because I have told you everything I heard from my Father.

You did not choose me; I chose you and appointed you to go and bear much fruit.

John 15:15–16

God has armed us with some powerful weapons, one of which is truth (see Ephesians 6:11–14). The right we have to assert such truths concerning who we are is a powerful weapon for defeating the enemy when he comes around.[2]

Avoiding Former Associations and Patterns

Clients need to be advised strongly against allowing themselves to get back into the same kinds of things their demons had attached themselves to in the past.

Many clients have belonged to formal or informal groups that have dragged them down through unwholesome friendships, often leading to harmful activities such as sexual immorality or misuse of drugs or alcohol. Belonging to secret societies (e.g., Freemasonry or college fraternities that require secret oaths) can be especially troublesome if not renounced.

Many clients have established patterns of behavior or places they frequent that expose them to strong temptations. The Internet is a problem for many, either due to a habit of looking at pornography or because of their involvement in online friendships. Certain kinds of movies and literature can be a problem as well.

Whatever the associations and behavior patterns, harmful habits need to be confronted, often by running away from tempting people, places and patterns. A male client seemed quite sincere about dealing with his attraction to men. After working with him in inner healing, however, he insisted on going to the fitness center where he had been greatly tempted and regularly fell. We dealt with his inner stuff and the demons attached to it, but he would not stay away from the place and people that tempted him. He seems to have given up; at least he has not come back to me for help for a couple of years.

Establishing Helpful Associations and Patterns

People who have been into destructive associations and patterns of behavior often need to develop friendships with people to whom they are accountable, friends who will help them fend off temptations and assist them if they fall. Some have found it helpful to have someone to report to daily or weekly in dealing with addictions to things like pornography, alcohol, drugs and smoking. The fear of letting their accountability partner down helps many people confront the power of their previous habits and establish new habits.

Counselees should also be advised to attend church services regularly, become part of a support group, and spend time privately with the Lord—memorizing Scripture and entering into worship via recorded worship music. The enemy does not like it when we glorify Jesus or associate with God's people, because when we do so we make a statement to the whole spirit universe concerning who we are and where our allegiance lies.

A particularly difficult situation is when a person is in constant contact with a spouse, relative or close friend whose very presence brings powerful temptation to return to the old patterns. Here, especially, the newly freed client needs at least one accountability partner with whom he or she can share deeply and go regularly to the throne of grace (see Hebrews 4:16) to lay new garbage at the feet of Jesus.

Working with Professional Counselors

Many people who have gone through deep-level healing find it helpful to work on their habits with professional counselors, especially if they have worked with them earlier. This can be quite beneficial, since professional counselors have learned how to help people change their habits. Working with a counselor before one is free can be frustrating; though counselees do receive help, there may be less real healing than they expected. Working with a counselor after one has gotten free, however, can be an entirely different experience.

I have worked with many clients who have spent years with professional counselors and have been disappointed with the results. People who are bound by powerful habits have great difficulty getting free without the Holy Spirit's help. If the counselor is working in a secular way, the client has only human power to work with, and that is seldom enough. After working with the Holy Spirit to gain freedom, however, the situation is quite different. Though the habits may be tough to break, coupling the freedom of the client with the expertise of the counselor can be very effective.

Now, Go Do It!

I have written this book in hopes that Christians can learn from it how to help people gain freedom and then maintain that freedom permanently. Following these guidelines, however, involves some risks—risks that the guidelines might not work or that we will run into a problem that is too big for us. Nevertheless, it is important to take such risks for at least three reasons.

1. *The only way we can learn is by* doing *this ministry.* We cannot learn to drive a car simply by spending time reading an instruction booklet. Though that is a good thing to do, unless we actually get behind the wheel and risk making mistakes, we will never learn to drive.

One of my mentors, John Wimber, used to say, "Faith is spelled R-I-S-K." I agree. John taught us to launch out in ministry and to keep at it, no matter how many times what we hoped would happen did not happen. God loves to heal, and I believe He loves to see us involved. When something good happens, then, we get to share in the blessing.

2. *A second reason for launching out is that there are multitudes upon multitudes of Christians who need the kind of freedom I am writing about.* Many people have come to faith but are living way below the level at which Jesus—and they themselves—wants them to be.

God's plan is for us to help each other. This is His "plan A," and I am convinced that He has no "plan B." Paul states this plan clearly in 2 Corinthians 1:4: "He helps us in all our troubles, so that we are able to help others who have all kinds of troubles, using the same help that we ourselves have received from God." If we do not help those in trouble, they probably will not receive help. God wants us to be in partnership with Jesus, who seldom does by Himself what He wants to get done. He wants us to share in the ministry and in the blessing. He wants those we help to be free and healed.

Imagine what our church experience would look like if we took 2 Corinthians 1:4 seriously and learned to help each other through deep-level healing. A church full of free people would look quite different than our churches do currently. I believe God would be very happy if deep-level healing were made a membership requirement in our churches.

3. *Yet another reason for taking the risk of ministry is that in working with Jesus to set captives free we enter into the enormous blessing of learning to participate with Him in His Kingdom program.* Thus, we discover, on the one hand,

who Jesus intends us to be and, on the other hand, who He wants to be to us.

Jesus actually shows up when we work with Him to set captives free. We, as well as our clients, experience His presence in unforgettable ways as we invite Him to come and work with us to do His will in the client's life. When He blesses our clients He blesses us, too, and we as well as they grow closer to Him.

Many of us who have taken the risks and have begun to minister deep-level healing to people have discovered that this ministry is not a matter of gifting or status. Anyone with a commitment to Jesus can do it. Jesus used rough Galilean fishermen to build His Church—fishermen who tested His patience continually with their doubting and lack of faith. If He could work with that bunch, He can certainly work with us.

I bless you who have read this book with a commitment to practicing deep-healing ministry and a closeness to Jesus that you have never had before.

Personal History Questionnaire

I ask each of my clients to fill out the following questionnaire, which I have used for many years and revised several times as my ministry developed.

This ministry is called *prayer ministry*. It is considered a form of *pastoral counseling*, not *professional counseling*. I am an ordained minister, not licensed as a professional counselor. I work with you only as you choose to work with me.

God has seen fit to work with and through me in moving people toward freedom from spiritual, emotional and even physical problems. It is, therefore, my expectation that He will help you through our time together. But I cannot control God or promise what He will do. I can only promise that I will do my best to work with God for your good and God's glory.

What usually happens in this type of ministry is that God brings a kind of "spurt" toward wholeness in each session. Sometimes additional work is necessary for a person to attain the complete freedom he or she and God desire. It may be advisable for the person to receive help from a professional counselor as well. I strongly advise this, especially in dealing with dysfunctional habits. It is always advisable for the person to actively pursue spiritual disciplines such as church attendance, prayer, Bible study and worship.

I am committed to keep confidential whatever you share with me. I am, however, *required by law* to report to appropriate persons two kinds of things:

1. Any intent of a person to take harmful, dangerous or criminal action against another person or against him- or herself, or
2. Any act of child or elderly abuse or neglect.

- *If it appears that such notification needs to be given, that intention will be shared with you first.*

In order to provide the appropriate legal protection, I ask that each person sign the following Statement of Release.

I hereby release Dr. Charles Kraft from any liability should this ministry session not live up to my expectations or lead to any spiritual, emotional or physical dysfunction.

_____   _____

Signed by Client   Date

_____   _____

Signed by Dr. Charles H. Kraft   Date

Personal History Questionnaire

Name _____

Address _____

Telephone _____ Occupation _____

Sex _____ Age _____ Education (highest grade) _____

How many older brothers _____ sisters _____ do you have?

How many younger brothers _____ sisters _____ do you have?

Were you adopted?   ☐Yes   ☐No

Were you brought up by someone other than your parents? Yes/No

If so, explain: _____

Did your parents want you? _____

Is it likely they were fighting while you were in the womb? _____

Was there a sense of security and harmony in your home during the first twelve years of your life? _____

How was authority exercised in the home? Which parent was in charge and how did he or she operate?

_____

_____

_____

How was affection shown between your parents and toward you?

_____

_____

_____

149

Marriage Information

Marital status _____

Name of spouse (if married) _____

Spouse's age _____ Occupation _____

Education (spouse's highest grade)_____

Date of marriage _____

Your ages when married: Husband _____ Wife _____

Have you ever been separated? ☐Yes   ☐No

If so, when? _____ For how long? _____

Have either of you ever filed for divorce?____ When?_____ Who?_____

Is your spouse willing to come for counseling? Yes No Uncertain

Give brief information about any previous marriages:

Information about Children

	Name	Age	Sex	Living (Yes/No)	Marital Status
1)					
2)					
3)					
4)					

Have you ever had a miscarriage? ☐Yes   ☐No

An abortion? ☐Yes   ☐No

Parents' Relationship

Is your father living? ☐Yes   ☐No

Is your mother living? ☐Yes   ☐No

Are your parents presently married to each other? ☐Yes   ☐No

Are you aware of any adultery and/or incest in your family or your grandparents' families? If so, explain. _____

_____

To your knowledge, have your parents, grandparents or great-grandparents ever been involved in any occult or non-Christian religious practices?

_____

_____

Briefly explain your parents' Christian experience (i.e., Did they profess to be Christians? If so, did they live out their Christianity?). _____

_____

_____

Family Health

Any addictions in your family (e.g., alcohol, drugs, gambling, eating disorders, etc.)? _____

Any history of mental or emotional illness? _____

Any history of any of the following?

☐ Tuberculosis   ☐ Heart disease   ☐ Diabetes   ☐ Cancer

☐ Ulcers   ☐ Glandular problems ☐ Epilepsy   ☐ Other: _____

Describe your family's concern for:

Diet _____ Exercise _____ Rest _____

Moral Climate

Rate the family atmosphere in each of the following areas during the first eighteen years of your life:

	Overly Permissive	Permissive	Average	Strict	Overly Strict
Clothing	5	4	3	2	1
Sex	5	4	3	2	1
Dating	5	4	3	2	1
Movies	5	4	3	2	1
Music	5	4	3	2	1
Reading material	5	4	3	2	1
Drinking	5	4	3	2	1
Smoking	5	4	3	2	1
Church attendance	5	4	3	2	1

Personality Information

Have you ever had any psychotherapy, counseling or prayer ministry?
☐ Yes   ☐ No

If yes, which? _____ When? _____

What was the outcome? _____

Circle any of the following words that describe you now:

active	nervous	moody	calm
ambitious	hardworking	often blue	serious
self-confident	impatient	excitable	easygoing
persistent	impulsive	imaginative	shy
introvert	good-natured	likeable	leader
extrovert	quiet	hard-boiled	submissive
sensitive	self-conscious	lonely	

Health Information

Physical:

Rate your health (circle): Very good   Good   Average   Declining   Poor

List all important present or past illnesses, injuries or handicaps:

_____

Date of last medical examination: _____ Report: _____

Are you presently taking medication?   ☐Yes   ☐No

If so, what? _____

Have you used drugs other than for medical purposes?   ☐Yes   ☐No

If so, what? _____

Describe your eating habits (i.e., Are you a junk food or health food addict? Do you eat regularly, or sporadically? Is your diet balanced?)

_____

Do you have addictions or cravings that you find difficult to control (food in general, sweets, drugs, alcohol, sex)?   ☐Yes   ☐No

If so, what? _____

Mental/Emotional:

Have you ever had a severe emotional upset? Yes/No

If so, explain: _____

Where would you put yourself on this optimism-pessimism scale?

Events: Pessimism 5 4 3 2 1 Optimism
                (i.e., things that happen tend to be bad/good)

People: Pessimism 5 4 3 2 1 Optimism
                (i.e., people tend to be evil/good)

Do you fear (or have you feared) that you might "crack up"?
☐Yes   ☐No

If so, explain: _____

Have you ever been arrested?   ☐Yes   ☐No

If so, why? _____

How much time do you spend per week watching TV? _____

How much time do you spend per week reading? What do you read?

_____

How much do you listen to music? What kind(s)? _____

Are you emotionally honest with God?   ☐Yes   ☐No

Explain: _____

Which of the following best describes how you handle positive and negative emotions?

☐ readily express all emotions   ☐ express some of my emotions but not all

☐ acknowledge their presence but reserved   ☐ tend to suppress my emotions

☐ find it safest not to express how I feel   ☐ tend to disregard how I feel since I can't trust my feelings

☐ consciously or subconsciously deny them since it is too painful to deal with some of them

Check and explain any problems with any of the following:

☐ Shame	☐ Hatred	☐ Fear	☐ Inadequacy
☐ Guilt	☐ Self-hatred	☐ Worry	☐ Unworthiness
☐ Deception	☐ Rejection	☐ Anxiety	☐ Insecurity
☐ Anger	☐ Self-rejection	☐ Panic	☐ Inferiority
☐ Bitterness	☐ Abandonment	☐ Lust	☐ Doubt
☐ Resentment	☐ Neglect	☐ Fantasy	☐ Skepticism
☐ Depression	☐ Death wish	☐ Pornography	☐ Pride
☐ Loneliness	☐ Suicidal thoughts	☐ Rebellion	☐ Obsessions
☐ Headaches	☐ Blasphemous thoughts		
☐ Compulsiveness	☐ Other: _____		

Religious Background

What church do you presently attend? _____

Who is the pastor? _____

Church attendance (times per month):   1 2 3 4 5 6 7 8 9 10+

Church you attended in childhood _____

Baptized?   ☐ Yes   ☐ No

Religious background of spouse (if married) _____

Do you know for certain that you will go to heaven when you die? Yes/No

What is your basis for answering the preceding question as you did?

_____

Are you plagued with doubts concerning your salvation?
☐ Yes   ☐ No

How much do you read the Bible?   Never   Occasionally   Often

How much time do you spend praying? Do you find praying difficult? How do you pray? Explain. _____

_____

Do you have a regular personal time with God? Yes/No

Do you have regular family devotions? Yes/No

When attending Christian meetings, are you plagued with foul thoughts, jealousies or other mental harassment? If so, explain.

_____

_____

Explain any recent changes in your religious life. _____

_____

155

Have you ever taken a class or read books on parapsychology or metaphysics or had other occult involvements? If so, explain. _____

_____

Have you ever heard voices in your mind? If so, explain. _____

_____

Describe any other experiences you may have had that would be considered out of the ordinary. _____

_____

Have you had any experience in the following cults and religions? If so, explain below.

Occult	Cults	Religions
☐ Astral projection	☐ Christian Science	☐ Zen Buddhism
☐ Ouija board	☐ Unity	☐ Hare Krishna
☐ Table tilting	☐ Scientology	☐ Bahai'ism
☐ Speaking in trance	☐ The Local Church	☐ Rosicrucianism
☐ Automatic writing	☐ The Way International	☐ Science of Mind
☐ Demonic dreams	☐ Unification Church	☐ Silva Mind Control
☐ Telepathy	☐ Unitarianism	☐ Eckankar
☐ Clairvoyance	☐ Jehovah's Witnesses	☐ Erhard Seminars
☐ Fortune-telling	☐ Children of God	☐ Transcendental meditation
☐ Tarot cards	☐ Mormonism	☐ Islam
☐ Healing magnetism	☐ Freemasonry/Eastern Star	☐ Black Muslim
☐ Palm reading	☐ New Age	☐ Hinduism
☐ Blood pacts	☐ Worldwide Church of God (Armstrong)	☐ Dowsing (rod or pendulum)
☐ Astrology	☐ Yoga	☐ Magic (black or white)
☐ Séances	☐ Amateur hypnosis	☐ Other: _____
☐ Going to psychics	☐ Theosophy	
☐ Games like Dungeons & Dragons		

_____

_____

Barriers to Freedom

Deception vs. Truth (study 1 John 1:5–2:2)

Are you aware that you have been believing any lies concerning life, yourself, others, etc.? _____

Are you aware of any of the following self-deceptions?
___Denial of reality
___Fantasy escape
___Attempts to identify self as someone else
___Emotional passivity
___Attempt to retreat to earlier stage of life
___Venting feelings on people weaker than those who hurt you

Are you given to defending yourself by any of the following?
___Covering up your weaknesses by overdoing your strengths
___Blaming others for your own problems
___Rationalization to justify yourself

Bitterness vs. Forgiveness (study Ephesians 4:31–32)

Ask God to bring to mind every relationship in which you have feelings of resentment or bitterness (including God), and list them.

_____

_____

_____

Ask God to reveal to you every person who needs to forgive you, and list them. _____

_____

_____

_____

157

Rebellion vs. Submission (study Romans 13:1–5)

Examine yourself with regard to any rebelliousness in relation to each of the following. Notice that each passage promises a blessing for a submissive response.

1. Civil government (1 Timothy 2:1–3; 1 Peter 2:13–17)
2. Parents (Ephesians 6:1–3)
3. Husband (1 Peter 3:1–6)
4. Employer (Ephesians 6:5–8; 1 Peter 2:18–21)
5. Church leaders (Hebrews 13:17)

Record any thoughts that come to you in this regard.

_____

_____

Pride vs. Humility (study James 4:6–10)

Examine yourself to see if you are consciously or unconsciously seeking your will more than God's. Record any thoughts that come to you in this regard.

_____

_____

Bondage vs. Freedom (study Galatians 5:1)

Examine yourself in the light of the following passages:

Romans 1:24–31	1 Corinthians 6:9–11
Galatians 5:19–21	Revelation 21:8; 22:15

Record any thoughts that come to your mind in this regard.

_____

_____

_____

Four Important Questions

How would you describe your problems?

_____

_____

_____

_____

What have you done about these problems?

_____

_____

_____

_____

What are your expectations in coming to us for ministry?

_____

_____

_____

_____

Is there any other information we should know?

_____

_____

_____

_____

Inner Healing Ministries

This listing is far from complete. Indeed, I have probably left out many ministries. I am certain that there are many churches and individuals that I don't know about (some of whom I have trained) who are doing inner healing. Still, I apologize for not including them.

The following list is a mixture of individuals, churches and an organization with over one hundred members in ministry—the International Society of Deliverance Ministers. This group, of which I am a member, has annual meetings (in September) and is growing. Though our announced focus is on deliverance, most (but not all) of our members recognize the importance of doing inner healing to dislodge demons.

I have given contact information as of February 2010. I have also given a very brief indication of the ministry focus of each person or group. For many of these there is more information on the internet. Much more information is available for many of these on their websites.

International Society of Deliverance Ministers—Janine Cave Emrick
Colorado Springs, Colorado
Organization of inner healing and deliverance ministers
www.deliveranceministers.org
isdm@globalharvest.org

Arlette Block
Switzerland
Training and individual ministry
arletteblock@yahoo.com

Ashland Theological Seminary—Terry Wardle, John Shultz
Ashland, Ohio
Seminars and degree programs in "formational counseling"
www.seminary.ashland.edu
Professor Terry Wardle: twardle@ashland.edu

Christian Healing Ministries—Francis and Judith MacNutt
Jacksonville, Florida
Teaching and individual ministry
www.christianhealingmin.org
lac@christianhealingmin.org
lhs@christianhealingmin.org

Cleansing Stream Ministries—Chris Hayward
Seminars, church-based ministry
www.cleansingstream.org

Deep Healing Ministries—Gary Hixson
Seville, Spain
Seminars and individual ministry
deephealing@gmail.com

Dream For God—Peter Rhee
Korea
Seminars and individual ministry
dream4god@kornet.net

Elijah House—John Sandford
Post Falls, Idaho (near Spokane, Washington)
Seminars and individual ministry
www.elijahhouse.org

Ellel Ministries USA
Lithia, Florida
A British ministry specializing in teaching subjects related to inner healing
www.ellelministries.org
infousa@ellelministries.org

Face2Face Ministries—Jimmy Stewart
Hong Kong
Individual ministry
face2faceministries@gmail.com

Freedom & Healing in Christ—Gary and Betsy Runkle-Edens
Pasadena, California
Individual ministry
www.freedomandhealinginchrist.org
freedomandhealing@earthlink.net

Freedom in Christ Ministries—Neil Anderson
Knoxville, Tennessee
Seminars
www.ficm.org

Grace Lutheran Church—Joe Johnson, counseling pastor
Huntington Beach, California
Individual ministry
jjohnson@gracehb.org

Hearts Set Free Ministries—Judy
Taber
Travels in the United States and Asia
Individual ministry and seminars
www.heartssetfree.org
judykaytaber@gmail.com

Hopkinton Vineyard—Rob Davis,
pastor
Hopkinton, Massachusetts
Individual ministry
www.vineyardhopkinton.org

Inverness Vineyard—Bubba Justice,
pastor
Birmingham, Alabama
Individual ministry
www.invernessvineyard.org

Peter Kang
Glendale, California
Seminars and individual ministry
(in English, Korean, Spanish,
Portuguese)
drpeterkang@gmail.com

Kraft Deep Healing Ministries—
Charles Kraft
Pasadena, California
Seminars and individual ministry
www.heartssetfree.org
ckraft@fuller.edu

Nehemiah Ministries—Felix Meier
Switzerland
Seminars and individual ministry
www.nehemia.net
felix.meier@nehemia.net

Restoration in Christ Ministries—
Tom Hawkins
Grottoes, Virginia
Seminars and individual ministry;
special focus on dissociative identity disorder
www.rcm-usa.org
tom@rcm-usa.org

Sandals Church—Nathan Brown, associate pastor
Riverside, California
Individual ministry
www.sandalschurch.com

Shepherd's House—James Wilder
Pasadena, California
Individual ministry
www.lifemodel.org

Solomon's Porch—Sam Song, pastor
Hong Kong
www.solomonsporchhk.com
Pastor Song: dunamis_ss@yahoo.com

Kathy Tschudin
Switzerland
Individual ministry
kaethy@solnet.ch

Notes

Chapter 1 Where Things Start

1. For more on this, see my book *Confronting Powerless Christianity* (Grand Rapids: Chosen, 2002).

2. See Siang-Yang Tan, *Lay Counseling* (Grand Rapids: Zondervan, 1991); Martin and Deidre Bobgan, *Psychoheresy: The Psychological Seduction of Christianity* (Santa Barbara, Calif.: Eastgate Publishers, 1987); Lakshman Madurasinghe, "Cognitive and Emotional Development of the Pre-born and Newly Born Baby," *Mum & Me*, November 2008.

Chapter 2 Problems to Deal With

1. I have treated this and other problems in detail in my book *Defeating Dark Angels* (Ventura, Calif.: Regal, 1992).

2. See Daniel Schacter, *Searching for Memory* (New York: Basic Books, 1996).

3. David Seamands, *Healing for Damaged Emotions* (Wheaton, Ill.: Victor, 1981), 155.

Chapter 3 How Things Are Stored: *Memories*

1. See Daniel Schacter, *Searching for Memory* (New York: Basic Books, 1996).

2. See Thomas Verny with John Kelly, *The Secret Life of the Unborn Child* (New York: Dell, 1982); Madurasinghe, "Cognitive and Emotional Development of the Pre-born and Newly Born Baby," *Mum & Me*, November 2008; and John T. Noonan, "The Experience of Pain by the Newborn," in Jeff Lane Hensley, *The Zero People* (Ann Arbor: Servant Publications, 1983).

3. Daniel Schacter, *Searching for Memory* (New York: Basic Books, 1996); Alan Baddeley, *Your Memory: A User's Guide* (Buffalo, N.Y.: Firefly Books, 2004).

4. Schacter, *Searching for Memory*.

5. David Seamands, *Healing for Damaged Emotions* (Wheaton, Ill.: Victor, 1981), 106.

Chapter 4 Our Inner Selves

1. For more on this subject, see chapter 11 of my book *Deep Wounds, Deep Healing* (Ventura, Calif.: Regal, 1993).

Chapter 5 Demonization

1. See Clinton E. Arnold, *Powers of Darkness: Principalities and Powers in Paul's Letters* (Grand Rapids: Zondervan, 1992).

2. See my book *Defeating Dark Angels* (Ventura, Calif.: Regal, 1992) for a more detailed discussion of this phenomenon.

3. John and Paula Sandford, *Healing the Wounded Spirit* (Tulsa, Okla.: Victory, 1985), 328.

4. C. Fred Dickason, *Demon Possession and the Christian* (Chicago: Moody, 1987).

5. Kraft, *Defeating Dark Angels*, 70.

6. John and Mark Sandford, *A Comprehensive Guide to Deliverance and Inner Healing* (Grand Rapids: Chosen, 1992), 112.

Chapter 7 Habits

1. For more on this concept of partnership, see my book *Confronting Powerless Christianity* (Grand Rapids: Chosen, 2002).

2. See my book *I Give You Authority* (Grand Rapids: Chosen, 1997) for more on this subject.

Bibliography

Anderson, Neil. *The Bondage Breaker.* Eugene, Ore.: Harvest House, 1990.

———. *Victory Over the Darkness.* Ventura, Calif.: Regal, 1990.

Arnold, Clinton E., *Powers of Darkness: Principalities and Powers in Paul's Letters.* Grand Rapids: Zondervan, 1992.

Baddeley, Alan. *Your Memory: A User's Guide.* Buffalo: Firefly Books, 2004.

Bennett, Rita. *Emotionally Free.* Old Tappan, N.J.: Fleming H. Revell, 1982.

———. *How to Pray for Inner Healing.* Old Tappan, N.J.: Fleming H. Revell, 1984.

———. *Making Peace with Your Inner Child.* Old Tappan, N.J.: Fleming H. Revell, 1987.

Blue, Ken. *Authority to Heal.* Downers Grove, Ill.: InterVarsity, 1987.

Bobgan, Martin, and Deidre Bobgan. *Psychoheresy: The Psychological Seduction of Christianity.* Santa Barbara, Calif.: Eastgate Publishers, 1987.

Bradshaw, John. *Healing the Shame That Binds You.* Deerfield Beach, Fla.: Health Communications, 1988.

Buhler, Rich. *Pain and Pretending.* Nashville: Thomas Nelson, 1991.

Capacchione, Lucia. *Recovery of Your Inner Child.* New York: Simon and Schuster, 1991.

Cole, Star. "What Is Memory Retrieval Like?" Based on material distributed privately by author. Anaheim: Hope and Restoration Ministries, 1992.

Dickason, C. Fred. *Demon Possession and the Christian.* Chicago: Moody, 1987.

Dickinson, Richard W., and Carole Gift Page. *The Child in Each of Us.* Wheaton: Victor, 1989.

Flynn, Mike. *Holy Vulnerability.* Old Tappan, N.J.: Fleming H. Revell, 1990.

Gibson, Noel, and Phyllis Gibson. *Evicting Demonic Squatters and*

Breaking Bondages. Drummoyne, NSW, Australia: Freedom in Christ Ministries, 1987.

Hammond, Frank D. *Overcoming Rejection.* Plainview, Tex.: The Children's Bread Ministries, 1987.

Harper, Michael. *Spiritual Warfare.* Ann Arbor: Servant Publications, 1984.

Hayford, Jack. *I'll Hold You in Heaven.* Ventura, Calif.: Regal, 1990.

Hensley, Jeff Lane. *The Zero People.* Ann Arbor: Servant Publications, 1983.

Horrobin, Peter. *Healing Through Deliverance.* 2 vols. Grand Rapids: Chosen, 2003.

Jacobs, Michael. *The Presenting Past.* New York: Harper and Row, 1985.

Kluft, Richard P., ed. *Childhood Antecedents of Multiple Personality.* Washington, D.C.: American Psychiatric Press, 1985.

Kraft, Charles H. *Christianity with Power.* Eugene, Ore.: Wipf & Stock, 2005.

———. *Confronting Powerless Christianity.* Grand Rapids: Chosen, 2002.

———. *Deep Wounds, Deep Healing.* Ventura, Calif.: Regal, 1993.

———. *Defeating Dark Angels.* Ventura, Calif.: Regal, 1992.

———. *I Give You Authority.* Grand Rapids: Chosen, 1997.

Linn, Dennis, and Matthew Linn. *Deliverance Prayer.* New York: Paulist, 1981.

———. *Healing the Greatest Hurt.* New York: Paulist, 1985.

———. *Healing Life's Hurts.* New York: Paulist, 1979.

———. *Healing of Memories.* New York: Paulist, 1984.

Littauer, Fred, and Florence Littauer. *Freeing Your Mind from Memories That Bind.* San Bernardino, Calif.: Here's Life Publishers, 1988.

MacNutt, Francis. *The Prayer That Heals.* Notre Dame, Ind.: Ave Maria, 1981.

MacNutt, Francis, and Judith MacNutt. *Praying for Your Unborn Child.* New York: Doubleday, 1988.

Madurasinghe, Lakshman, "Cognitive and Emotional Development of the Pre-born and Newly Born Baby." *Mum & Me,* November 2008.

Matzat, Don. *Inner Healing: Deliverance or Deception?* Eugene, Ore.: Harvest House, 1987.

McCall, Kenneth. *Healing the Family Tree.* London: Sheldon Press, 1982.

McDonald, Robert L. *Memory Healing.* Atlanta: RLM Ministries, Inc., 1981.

Murphy, Ed. "From My Experience: My Daughter Demonized?" *Equipping the Saints* 4, no. 1 (Winter 1990): 27–29.

———. *Handbook for Spiritual Warfare.* Nashville: Thomas Nelson, 1992.

Noonan, John T. "The Experience of Pain by the Newborn." In Jeff Lane Hensley, *The Zero People,* Ann Arbor: Servant Publications, 1983.

Payne, Leanne. *The Broken Image.* Westchester, Ill.: Crossway, 1981.

———. *The Healing Presence.* Westchester, Ill.: Crossway, 1989.

Powell, John. *Why Am I Afraid to Love?* Niles, Ill.: Argus Communications, 1975.

Pytches, Mary. *A Child No More*. London: Hodder and Stoughton, 1991.

———. *A Healing Fellowship*. London: Hodder and Stoughton, 1988.

———. *Set My People Free*. London: Hodder and Stoughton, 1987.

———. *Yesterday's Child*. London: Hodder and Stoughton, 1990.

Reed, William S. *Healing of the Whole Man—Mind, Body, Spirit*. Old Tappan, N.J.: Spire Books, 1979.

Rowan, John. *Subpersonalities: The People Inside Us*. New York: Routledge, 1990.

Sandford, John, and Mark Sandford. *A Comprehensive Guide to Deliverance and Inner Healing*. Grand Rapids: Chosen, 1992.

Sandford, John, and Paula Sandford. *God's Power to Change*. Lake Mary, Fla.: Charisma House, 2007.

———. *Healing the Wounded Spirit*. Tulsa: Victory, 1985.

———. *The Transformation of the Inner Man*. South Plainfield, N.J.: Bridge, 1982.

———. *Transforming the Inner Man*. Lake Mary, Fla.: Charisma House, 2007.

Sandford, Paula. *Healing Victims of Sexual Abuse*. Tulsa: Victory, 1988.

Sandford, R. Loren. *Wounded Warriors: Surviving Seasons of Stress*. Tulsa: Victory, 1987.

Sanford, Agnes. *The Healing Gifts of the Spirit*. Old Tappan, N.J.: Revell, 1966.

Scanlan, Michael. *Inner Healing*. New York: Paulist, 1974.

Schacter, Daniel L. *Searching for Memory: The Brain, the Mind, and the Past*. New York: Basic Books, 1996.

Schwartz, Richard. "Our Multiple Selves." *The Family Therapy Networker* (March–April 1987): 25–31, 80–83.

Seamands, David A. *Healing for Damaged Emotions*. Wheaton: Victor, 1981.

———. *Healing Grace*. Wheaton: Victor, 1988.

———. *Healing of Memories*. Wheaton: Victor, 1985.

———. *Putting Away Childish Things*. Wheaton: Victor, 1982.

———. *Redeeming the Past*. Wheaton: Victor, 1985.

Smedes, Lewis B. *Caring and Commitment*. San Francisco: Harper and Row, 1988.

———. *Forgive and Forget*. San Francisco: Harper and Row, 1984.

Stanford, Susan. *Will I Cry Tomorrow?* Old Tappan, N.J.: Revell, 1987.

Stapleton, Ruth. *The Experience of Inner Healing*. Waco, TX: Word, 1977.

———. *The Gift of Inner Healing*. Waco: Word, 1976.

Tan, Siang-Yang. *Lay Counseling*. Grand Rapids: Zondervan, 1991.

Tapscott, Betty. *Inner Healing Through Healing of Memories*. Kingwood, Tex.: Hunter Publishing, 1987.

———. *Ministering Inner Healing Biblically*. Houston: Tapscott Ministries, 1987.

Verny, Thomas, with John Kelly. *The Secret Life of the Unborn Child*. New York: Dell, 1982.

Wardle, Terry. *Healing Care, Healing Prayer*. Orange, Calif.: New Leaf, 2001.

White, Thomas B. *The Believer's Guide to Spiritual Warfare*. Ann Arbor: Servant Publications, 1990.

Whitfield, Charles L. *Healing the Child Within*. Deerfield Beach, Fla.: Health Communications, 1987.

Wilson, Sandra. *Released from Shame*. Downers Grove, Ill.: InterVarsity, 1990.

Wimber, John. *Power Healing*. San Francisco: Harper and Row, 1987.

Index

Since 1969, **Charles (Chuck) Kraft** has been professor of anthropology and intercultural communication in the School of Intercultural Studies (formerly the School of World Mission) at Fuller Seminary in Pasadena, California. Chuck teaches anthropology, communication, contextualization and spiritual dynamics (inner healing, deliverance and spiritual warfare). He is also the president of Kraft Deep Healing Ministries, conducting seminars in the United States and around the world on deep-level (inner) healing, deliverance and spiritual warfare.

Chuck holds degrees from Wheaton College (B.A. in anthropology), Ashland Theological Seminary (B.D. in theology) and Hartford Seminary Foundation (Ph.D. in anthropological linguistics). He served as a pioneer missionary among a tribal group (Kamwe) in northeastern Nigeria for three years, followed by five years each on the faculties of Michigan State University (1963–1968) and UCLA (1968–1973), where he taught linguistics and African languages before moving to Fuller in 1969. He and his wife, Marguerite, have four children, fifteen grandchildren and one great-grandchild.

This is Chuck's thirtieth book. He has written books and articles in each of the areas in which he has taught, including the books *Christianity in Culture*; *Communication Theory for Christian Witness*; *Communicating Jesus' Way*; *Anthropology for Christian Witness*; *Worldview for Christian Witness*; *Appropriate Christianity*; *Christianity with Power*; *Deep Wounds, Deep Healing*; *Defeating Dark Angels*; *The Rules of Engagement*; *Confronting Powerless Christianity* and *I Give You Authority*.

Chuck may be contacted by email at ckraft@fuller.edu or chkmeg@gmail.com.